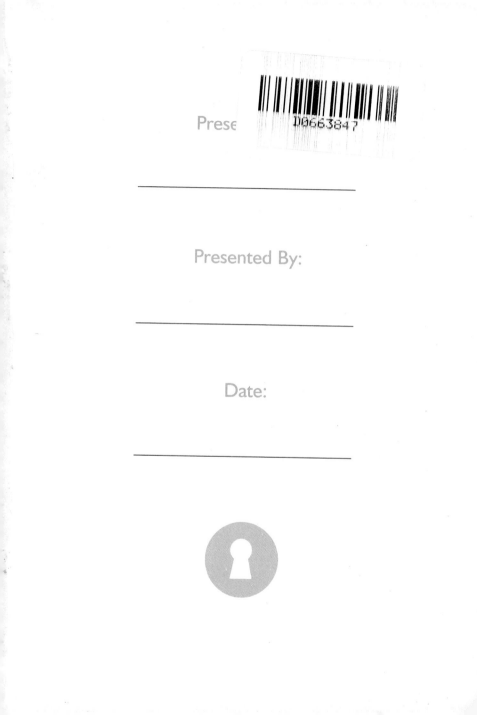

Prese   D0663847

_____

Presented By:

_____

Date:

_____

words

to live by
for teens

Unlock the POWER of Words to
Change Your Life Forever

words

to live by
for teens

Reflections & Insights on the
Most Life-Changing & Thought-
Provoking Words in the Bible

BETHANYHOUSE

Words to Live By for Teens
ISBN 0-7642-2924-9

Copyright © 2004 by GRQ, Inc.
Brentwood, Tennessee 37027

Published by Bethany House Publishers
11400 Hampshire Avenue South
Bloomington, Minnesota 55438
www.bethanyhouse.com

Bethany House Publishers is a division of Baker Publishing Group, Grand Rapids, Michigan.

Scripture quotations noted GNT are taken from GOOD NEWS TRANSLATION, SECOND EDI-
TION, Copyright (c) 1992 by the American Bible Society. Used by permission. All rights reserved.

Scripture quotations noted CEV are taken from The Contemporary English Version. © 1991 by the
American Bible Society. Used by permission.

Scripture quotations noted GOD'S WORD are taken from GOD'S WORD. GOD'S WORD is a copy-
righted work of God's Word to the Nations Bible Society. Quotations are used by permission.
Copyright 1995 by God's Word to the Nations Bible Society. All rights reserved.

Scripture quotations noted KJV are taken from the King James Version.

Scripture quotations noted THE MESSAGE are taken from THE MESSAGE: The New Testament,
Psalms and Proverbs. Copyright © 1993, 1994, 1995 by Eugene H. Peterson. All rights reserved.

Scripture quotations noted NASB are taken from the New American Standard Bible® Copyright ©
1960, 1962, 1963–1968, 1971, 1973–1975, 1977, 1995 by the Lockman Foundation. Used by
permission.

Scripture quotations noted NCV are taken from The Holy Bible, New Century Version, copyright ©
1987, 1988, 1991 by Word Publishing, Dallas, Texas 75039. Used by permission.

Scripture quotations noted NIV are taken from the *Holy Bible: New International Version* (North
American Edition)®. Copyright © 1973–1978, 1984, by the International Bible Society. Used by
permission of Zondervan. All rights reserved.

Scripture quotations noted NKJV are taken from The New King James Version. Copyright © 1979,
1980, 1982, Thomas Nelson, Inc., Publishers.

Scripture quotation noted NLT are taken from the *Holy Bible*, New Living Translation, copyright ©
1996. Used by permission of Tyndale House Publishers, Inc., Wheaton, Illinois 60189. All rights
reserved.

Scripture quotations noted NRSV are taken from the New Revised Standard Version of the Bible,
copyright © 1989 by the Division of Christian Education of the National Council of the Churches of
Christ in the USA. Used by permission. All rights reserved.

All rights reserved. No part of this publication may be reproduced, stored in a retrieval system, or
transmitted in any form or by any means—electronic, mechanical, photocopying, recording, or any
other—without the prior written permission of the publisher and copyright owner.

Library of Congress Control Number 2004010924

Compiler and Editor: Lila Empson
Writer: J. Heyward Rogers
Design: Whisner Design Group

Printed in the United States of America. All rights reserved under International Copyright Law.
Contents and/or cover may not be reproduced in whole or in part in any form without the express
written consent of the publisher.

04 05 06 / 4 3 2

The life-maps of GOD are
right, showing the way to joy.
The directions of GOD are
plain and easy on the eyes.

Psalm 19:8 THE MESSAGE

Contents

Introduction

When Jesus talked about what God is like, and what it's like to know him, he offered up images that you can see in your mind's eye—a treasure buried in a field, a camel struggling to squeeze through the eye of a needle, a father running down the road to embrace his long-lost son.

And yet when people talk about what the Bible says, the words suddenly leave the real world of sights, sounds, and smells, and become abstract. They talk about holiness, repentance, belief, humility. The life of faith begins to sound like a list of concepts rather than something you live. If you go to church, you hear these words so often that you might forget what they mean.

words
to live by

You don't live in a world of concepts. You live in a world of people, places, things, actions. You live in a world of term papers, pizzas, rehearsals, parents, after-school jobs. But that doesn't mean the concepts aren't relevant to your life. God calls you to be holy; you need to know what holiness is. He offers peace; you need to know what that is too.

The purpose of this book is to take sixty biblical concepts and lasso them down from the realm of abstraction to the world where you live. You'll see how hope is like wearing braces, how Christian liberty is like having a driver's license. You'll get ideas for applying biblical truths to your life. And hopefully you'll see that these aren't just words. They're words to live by.

I believe in Christianity as I believe
that the sun has risen, not only
because I see it, but because by it
I see everything else.

O

C. S. Lewis

a·bun·dance, noun

1. an ample quantity; profusion.
2. affluence, wealth.
3. a relative degree of plentifulness.
4. *Biblical:* an exceeding measure; something above the ordinary; describes both the power of God and God's overflowing spiritual gifts and spiritual fruits.
5. *Personal:* God's goodness spilling over in the lives of his people.

God's Overflow

I came that they may have life,
and have it abundantly.
John 10:10 NASB

God has a habit of over-delivering when his people look to him to meet their needs. When Jesus fed the five thousand, he didn't give them just enough to get by. Everyone ate until they were satisfied, and there were twelve full baskets of leftovers. When he filled the disciples' fishing nets after a long night's unsuccessful work, the boat nearly sank with the excess. Jesus said he came to give abundant life. That's what he was talking about: a life in which the gifts of God overflow and spill out all over the place.

You've heard the saying "Give a person an inch, and he'll take a yard." One of the awesome things about God is that when you ask him for an inch, he gives you a mile. The woman at the well came looking for a drink of water, but she ran into Jesus there and came away with Living Water: "Whoever drinks of the water that I will give him," promised Jesus, "shall never thirst; but the water

words
to live by

that I will give him will become in him a well of water springing up to eternal life" (John 4:14 NASB).

The things of earth, if they fill you at all, fill you only temporarily. Earthly water quenches your thirst, but it won't be long before you're thirsty again. Earthly food can ease your hunger, but you'll get hungry again. The fullness of a life in which God reigns is a fullness that overflows today, tomorrow, and forever. When the limitless goodness of God is poured into a human life, it's more than can be contained. Not only are you filled up, but the blessings of God, as they overflow, are spilled onto the people around you.

> God sends no one away empty except those who are full of themselves.
>
> DWIGHT L. MOODY

You can try to fill yourself up with activities, accomplishments, popularity—there are lots of ways to work at self-fulfillment. But your bucket has a hole in it; earthly fulfillment leaks out the bottom as fast as you can heap it in the top. In the book of Jeremiah, God compares that kind of life to the dirty, difficult work of digging a cistern: "They have forsaken me—the fountain of living water. And they have dug for themselves cracked cisterns that can hold no water at all!" (Jeremiah 2:13 NLT). A cistern was a big hole in the ground for collecting rainwater for drinking. Who would do the backbreaking work of digging a leaky cistern when anyone could dip water out of a bubbling spring? For that matter, who would drink warm, scummy rainwater when a person could have fresh, cold spring water?

The abundant life that God offers in Christ bubbles forth like a fountain. It never runs dry. It never even gets low. You don't have to earn it or work for it any more than you have to earn the sunlight that shines down on you every day. Here is acceptance, security, peace, fellowship, joy, satisfaction, fulfillment—all those things you strive for in your own efforts. Scoop it up. Drink deeply. Take more than you need. There's plenty more where that came from.

> You will show me the path that leads to life; your presence fills me with joy and brings me pleasure forever.
> Psalm 16:11 GNT

do something

Are you too busy for abundance? A full schedule isn't the same thing as a full life. If your days are overflowing with activity, it can be hard to enjoy the overflowing blessings that Jesus called the abundant life. Slow down. Make time to pray, to read, to meditate on the promises of the God who offers abundant life.

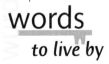

words
to live by

However many blessings we expect from God, His infinite liberality will always exceed all our wishes and our thoughts.

JOHN CALVIN

My God will supply all your needs according to His riches in glory in Christ Jesus.

Philippians 4:19 NASB

The prophet Jeremiah had double reason to prefer springs over cisterns. His neighbors, tired of hearing his prophecies, once threw him into a muddy cistern and left him to die. He was rescued when a servant ran and told King Zedekiah what had happened.

The Greek word used to describe the twelve baskets of leftovers when Jesus fed the five thousand—that is, the overabundance of food—is the same word Jesus used when he spoke of abundant life. In other words, he's offering you all the life you want, with more left over.

final thought

God, you are infinite and supply my needs according to your riches. Thank you that when I ask for daily bread you sit me down to a feasting table. Amen.

a·dop·tion, noun

1. choosing or taking as one's own.
2. becoming the legal parent or parents of (another person's child).
3. accepting another into a close, dependent relationship.
4. **Biblical:** God's acceptance of believers as his sons and daughters.
5. **Personal:** The privilege of calling God "Father."

Who Art in Heaven

The Spirit makes you God's children, and by the Spirit's power we cry out to God, "Father! my Father!"
Romans 8:15 GNT

You already know that God is your Father. You say it every time you say the Lord's Prayer: "Our Father, who art in heaven, hallowed be thy name . . ." In fact, God's father-nature is such a common idea, you may have never given five minutes' thought to what it means. But God's relating to believers as a Father to his children is at the very heart of the Christian life.

Have you ever called God "Daddy"? The apostle Paul did. "For you have not received a spirit of slavery which leads to fear again, but you have received a spirit of adoption as sons by which we cry out 'Abba! Father!'" (Romans 8:15 NASB). That word *abba* means "Daddy" or "Papa." A man can be a father without having a relationship with his child. But he can't be a daddy. The word *daddy* speaks of a personal relationship, a loving relationship. It speaks of a child who looks to the father for everything. It speaks of a

words
to live by

child who wants more than anything to please the father. It speaks of a child who is not ashamed to ask for anything. It speaks of a child who has nothing to fear.

When God adopts you as a son or daughter, it's a forever thing. You have all the rights, all the privileges, all the security of natural-born sons and daughters. Through good times and bad, throughout life and throughout eternity, you have a Father who loves you and meets your every need. And you have an inheritance: eternal, abundant life.

Snuggle in God's arms. When you are hurting, when you feel lonely, left out . . . let Him cradle you, comfort you, reassure you of His all-sufficient power and love.

KAY ARTHUR

Consider what happens to a child who is taken out of an orphanage and adopted into a loving home. A child with no future suddenly has a future, even an inheritance. And the child has done nothing to earn this new status. Nor can the child do anything to lose it. An adopted child can't be un-adopted.

But adoption doesn't end with the "adoption process" any more than marriage ends with a wedding ceremony. When parents have finally finished the long, rigorous process of adopting a baby and have the signed adoption papers, they don't leave the baby at the orphanage. "Have a nice life, kid. And remember, if anybody asks, we're your parents. It says so right here on these legal documents." Of course not. The legal process is just the beginning of adoption. The parents take the baby home, meet every need, love the baby into the family. The adoption papers make them officially mother and father. It's the life of a loving household that makes them mommy and daddy. In the same way, God's adoption is about a relationship, not just a new legal status. It's not just that God declares you to be a son or daughter, but that he loves you as a son or daughter, and you love him as a Father for an eternity.

When you are in Christ, you find yourself in the most astonishing, the most marvelous, the most inexplicable situation: The Maker of heaven and earth cradles you in his loving arms and asks you to call him Daddy. The tender gaze of the Father makes all fears melt away. His gaze gives you a hope and an inheritance of eternal life. And it cannot be taken away.

> As many as received Him, to them He gave the right to become children of God.
> John 1:12 NASB

do something

Never forget that you are the child of a King! God is a loving Father who will always meet your needs and who will someday welcome you into the fullness of your inheritance in heaven. When times are hard at school or at home, rest in the arms of God, who has adopted you as his child.

words
to live by

God walks with us. . . . He scoops us up in His arms or simply sits with us in silent strength until we cannot avoid the awesome recognition that yes, even now, He is there.
GLORIA GAITHER

The Spirit Himself testifies with our spirit that we are children of God, and if children, heirs also, heirs of God and fellow heirs with Christ, if indeed we suffer with Him so that we may also be glorified with Him.
Romans 8:16–17 NASB

Though it was quite common among the Greeks and Romans, adoption was rare among the Jews. Of all New Testament writers, Paul had the closest ties to Greek and Roman culture. Perhaps that's why he's the only New Testament writer who describes the believer's relationship to God in terms of adoption.

In the Roman Empire, adults were adopted more often than children. Wealthy persons with no heirs would sometimes adopt a worthy adult in order to have someone to leave their estate to. Under Roman law, an adoptee could never be disowned by their adoptive parent.

final thought

God, you are the great Father. You are my great Father, my heavenly Daddy, and I celebrate the love that caused you to adopt me as your child. Don't let me forget that I am your child forever. Amen.

an·gel, noun

1. a spiritual being superior to humans in power and intelligence.
2. an attendant spirit or guardian.
3. a messenger, especially of God.
4. *Biblical:* a superhuman or heavenly being who serves as God's messenger and acts to fulfill God's will.
5. *Personal:* a heavenly agent, always at work carrying out God's purposes on earth.

God's Secret Agents

Praise the LORD, you his angels,
you mighty ones who do his bidding,
who obey his word.
Psalm 103:20 NIV

What would happen if an angel, in full glory, made an appearance in your school cafeteria? There you are, just minding your business, eating your lunch, when a blinding light fills the room. All around you, hundreds of forks clatter onto lunchroom trays as everyone in the cafeteria is overcome with astonishment at such a spectacle.

What would you feel? It's likely that the first thing you'd feel is fear. When angels show up in the Bible, people are usually terrified. Before the angels can do the work they've come to do, they first have to calm the fears of the human beings who cower before them, stunned by their brightness. "Peace! Do not be afraid. You are not going to die"; "Do not be afraid, O man highly esteemed. Peace! Be strong; be strong"; "Do not be afraid, Mary"; "Do not be afraid. I bring you good news of great joy." But soon the people of

words
to live by

God are comforted—and, more than comforted, they are overjoyed to see that such powerful beings as these are working on their behalf.

On the other hand, it's possible that an angel could pay a visit and nobody would notice. The angel slips in, performs the assigned mission, and then slips away, like a spy of heaven. The Bible makes it clear that people do sometimes interact with angels without even realizing it (Hebrews 13:2).

There seems to be a renewed interest in angels lately. They show up in movies and television shows, on posters, in little statuettes that people decorate their rooms with. But you have to wonder what the angels think about this popular interest in all things angelic. In the first place, they may feel a little insulted. Compare the immensely powerful, terrifyingly bright beings of the Bible to some of the angels you see in pop culture. There are many different kinds of angels in the Bible, but none of them are pudgy little babies fluttering around with a sweet smile on their face. They're doing serious work. They manifest the awesome power of God unleashed on behalf of God's people.

> Angels are a reality, and this should be a great comfort to us. But we do not worship them. Only Christ is worthy of our worship, for only He died to take away our sins.
> **BILLY GRAHAM**

The Bible is very clear: Angels are real, and they are an important part of God's plan for working out his will on earth. They protect God's people from forces you can't even see. But they act at God's bidding, not at the bidding of human beings. Another thing the Bible makes clear is that angels always direct

jilness grace mercy love hand goodness truth succor holy
jorgiveness peace humble holiness obey repent perfect submit
erve fellowship comforter transformed noble character church

an·gel · an·gel · an·gel · an·gel · an·gel · an·gel

attention away from themselves and toward God and the things of God. They are the most faithful of servants—too faithful, even, to willingly take your focus off the God they serve. In several places throughout the Bible, humans bow down and try to worship the angels who appear to them. It's an understandable mistake; to mortal eyes, a being who is so bright and so overwhelming must look like a god. But in every case, the angels are quick to correct the worshiper: "Not so fast," they always say. "I'm just the messenger. You should see the One who sent me!"

> I fell down at the feet of the angel who had shown me these things, and I was about to worship him. But he said to me, "Don't do it! I am a servant together with you and with your brothers the prophets and of all those who obey the words in this book. Worship God!"
> **Revelation 22:8–9** GNT

do something

The Bible says that God gives his angels charge over you, to guard you in everything you do. They aren't little naked babies flying around you, or a little guy in white robes and wings sitting on your shoulder like in the cartoons. The angels who look out for you are truly awe-inspiring creatures. In your spiritual battles, they are mighty warriors.

words
to live by

The angel of the LORD encamps around those who fear Him, and rescues them.
Psalm 34:7 NASB

By and large we should probably leave it to God how he will use angels to get his work done. If God shows us more, we will use it. But the essence of the matter is not knowing the spirits but knowing God and praying in the power of Holy Spirit.
John Piper

A physicist named Dr. Phil Schewe calculated that 1,025 angels can dance on the point of a pin. He wasn't exactly serious, but his calculations combined quantum physics with the angelology of the medieval theologian Thomas Aquinas.

Angels, performing many different functions, are mentioned almost three hundred times in the Bible. But only two of those angels are identified by name: Gabriel, who announced the birth of Jesus, and Michael, who leads the angel armies against the Beast in Revelation.

Final thought

Thank you, God, for the angels that encamp around me for my protection and for your glory. Like them, may I always point others toward the God I serve. Amen.

ness grace mercy love faith goodness truth freedom hope
orgiveness peace humble holiness obey repent perfect submit
erve fellowship comforter transformed noble character church

as·sur·ance, noun

1. security.
2. being certain in the mind.
3. confidence of mind or manner; easy freedom from self-doubt or uncertainty.
4. **Biblical:** the confidence of Christians that they are children of God and heirs of heaven.
5. **Personal:** a trust in God's mercy.

Jerusalem, I can never forget you! I have written your name on the palms of my hands.
Isaiah 49:16 GNT

If you're in Christ, your name is written on God's hands. It's not written in ballpoint; it's not a temporary reminder, the way you might write "biology test Monday" on the palm of your hand so you don't forget to study. No, the word translated *written* in the verse quoted above is really more like *engraved* or *tattooed*. The names of God's people can't be scrubbed away. For all eternity, they're right there in God's sight, where he can't miss them.

Here's something that will boggle your mind: If you are in Christ, your future, your eternity is just as secure as that of the saints who are already in heaven. They're happier than you are; they don't have to think about final exams or dating or their wardrobe. They don't have to deal with worry or doubts or temptation. But they aren't more secure than you are.

words
to live by

You are in the grip of grace. There's no prying the fingers of the loving Christ away from you. "I am convinced," wrote the apostle Paul, "that neither death nor life, neither angels nor demons, neither the present nor the future, nor any powers, neither height nor depth, nor anything else in all creation, will be able to separate us from the love of God that is in Christ Jesus our Lord" (Romans 8:38–39 NIV).

Cling to Christ. Hold on to your Savior with all the strength you can muster. But when your grasp starts to slip (and it will), know that your security comes from God's grip on you, not your grip on him. That's what assurance means; it's a confidence that the God who has called you to himself is faithful to keep you. In spite of your failures. In spite of your doubts.

> Christ never fails of success. Christ never undertakes to heal any but he makes a certain cure. . . . Other physicians can only cure them that are sick, but Christ cures them that are dead.
> **THOMAS WATSON**

One of the great benefits of this assurance is the joy it brings; it's a good feeling. But sometimes you just don't feel all that good. You don't feel secure. You don't feel like the apple of God's eye. What then? That's when you take your eyes off yourself—your mistakes, your doubt, your self-pity—and look to the God who loved you so much he gave up his Son for you.

The concept of *assurance* has two components: the feeling of assurance or security, and the fact of your assurance. The facts don't change, even though your feelings do. Losing the

as·sur·ance · as·sur·ance · as·sur·ance

feeling of assurance isn't the same thing as losing your salvation. It's all the more reason to turn back to the God who has both the power and the desire to restore you to himself.

Assurance—the security of knowing that you are in the palm of God's hand both now and throughout eternity—is a little glimpse of what you have to look forward to in heaven. Apart from God, there's nothing really sure in this earthly existence. But the assurance you have in Christ lifts you above the uncertainties of day-to-day life and gives you rest and confidence in the unfailing mercies of God, who never changes.

> I am not ashamed; for I know whom I have believed and I am convinced that He is able to guard what I have entrusted to Him until that day.
>
> **2 Timothy 1:12** NASB

do something

In the ups and downs of life, your feelings are constantly changing. That's just as true for your feeling of assurance as it is for any other feeling. Sometimes you feel spiritually secure, and sometimes you don't. When your feelings of assurance or spiritual security begin to fail, take a step back and focus on the facts of God's faithfulness. The feelings will follow.

words
to live by

The love I bear Christ is but a faint and feeble spark, but it is an emanation from himself: He kindled it and he keeps it alive; and because it is his work, I trust many waters shall not quench it.

JOHN NEWTON

If we are unfaithful, he remains faithful, for he cannot deny himself.
2 Timothy 2:13 NLT

ᴛᴛ One of the words translated as *assurance* in the New Testament literally means "fullness" or "abundance"—in other words, the life of surety is a life that's filled to the top, even overflowing. Assurance is closely related to the concept of abundance.

ᴛᴛ In the Middle Ages, pilgrims who made journeys to the Holy Land sometimes tattooed pictures of the walls of Jerusalem on the backs of their hands. They took the idea from Isaiah 49:16. Like God's metaphorical hand-tattoo, the pilgrims' physical tattoos were a constant reminder of Jerusalem.

final thought

God, you always keep your promises. My assurance, my security comes from your sure grip on me, not my grip on you. As I go through this day, I pray that I would know the assurance that comes from relying on your faithfulness. Amen.

God's Tattoo

oness grace mercy love faith goodness truth freedom hope
orgiveness peace humble holiness obey repent perfect submit
erve fellowship comforter transformed noble character church

beau·ty, noun

1. loveliness.
2. a particularly graceful, ornamental, or excellent quality.
3. a person or thing that excels or is remarkable of its kind.
4. *Biblical:* the rightness or appropriateness of a thing or person that gives pleasure to the mind or the senses.
5. *Personal:* the loveliness of God, which becomes the believers' own loveliness as God makes them more and more like Christ.

God's Loveliness

Honor and majesty surround him;
strength and beauty are in his sanctuary.
Psalm 96:6 NLT

In the old bedtime story, the first time the Ugly Duckling saw a flock of swans, he was gripped by a feeling he couldn't explain. He had spent his whole life in a cold and ugly world where he didn't fit in—a world that had convinced him that he was the ugly one. Then, one cold autumn evening, he was dazzled by the sight of a whole flock of great, graceful, white birds flying south to warmer lands. As he watched them soar in the sky, the Duckling was gripped with a strange joy that he couldn't explain. He didn't know what these majestic birds were, but he loved them more than he had ever loved anything.

Though he didn't know it at the time, the swans' beauty spoke to him of his true home, his true self. For he was one of them, destined to be that beautiful, to fly that high, even if the world had convinced him otherwise.

words
to live by

Why do human beings crave beauty? What is that vague longing you feel when you see a majestic mountain range or hear a beautiful piece of music or see a baseball field that has just been mowed? Maybe it's a homing instinct. John Piper wrote, "God is the ultimately Beautiful One, and he made us to long for himself." There's ugliness in this fallen world. But when you get a glimpse of beauty, of excellence, you feel in your bones that you were made for something better. At some level, the longing for beauty is a longing for God.

When you think something is beautiful, you gaze at it. You can't help it. You don't yawn and look away the first time you see an eagle in flight. You stare until the great bird is out of sight. How about God? Do you find him beautiful? There's no other beauty so satisfying. The beauty of a sunset points you toward the majesty of God, but once you begin to see the beauties of God himself, sunsets and super-models pale by comparison.

As you gaze on God's beauty, you become beautiful yourself. Your beauty will finally be completed in heaven, when you look God full in the face. "What we will be has not yet been made known. But we know that when he appears, we shall be like him, for we shall see him as he is" (1 John 3:2 NIV).

While he still lived among the ducks, the Duckling's true self was still unknown. But at last he mustered the courage to

> People are like stained-glass windows. They sparkle and shine when the sun is out, but when the darkness sets in, their true beauty is revealed only if there is a light from within.
>
> **ELISABETH KUBLER-ROSS**

join the swans, and, to his amazement, the swans welcomed him. He discovered that he had been a swan from the start. And his life among the ducks seemed a distant dream.

Do you ever feel like an Ugly Duckling? Do you ever feel that you just don't fit into your world? There's a good reason why: Ultimately, this world isn't what you were made for. You may or may not possess the superficial beauty that is prized in this culture. You may look like an ugly duckling, or you may look like an attractive duckling, but in the end, you aren't a duckling at all. You're a swan. And your true self—the self that is being shaped day by day until it is finally completed in heaven—is far too beautiful for this world.

> Your eyes will see the King in His beauty; they will see the land that is very far off.
>
> Isaiah 33:17 NKJV

do something

The Bible is clear: Beauty is a good thing. The yearning it creates is a faint echo of God's beauty. But if you mistakenly believe that any earthly beauty can fulfill you—if you don't let that longing point you to the One you truly long for—then the beauty of earthly things becomes a vain and empty thing.

words
to live by

He has made every-
thing beautiful in its
time. He has also set
eternity in the hearts of
men; yet they cannot
fathom what God has
done from beginning
to end.
Ecclesiastes 3:11 NIV

Give beauty back, beau-
ty, beauty, beauty, back
to God, beauty's self
and beauty's giver.
GERARD MANLEY HOPKINS

Ancient beauty secrets included
face cream made out of the sweat
and dirt extracted from sheep's
wool, and eye liner made up of a
mixture of bear fat and lamp soot.

How much did King David
value beauty? Out of his own
wealth, he gave 110 tons of gold
and 260 tons of silver for the dec-
oration of the temple in Jerusalem.
Today, that much gold and silver
would be worth about a billion
dollars.

Final thought

God, give me eyes to see your beauty. Give me a heart that longs
for your beauty, that follows all earthly beauty to its true source,
the beauty of its Creator. And as I look into your face, God, may I
become more beautiful too. Amen.

be·lief, noun

1. a confidence in the truth or existence of something not immediately susceptible to rigorous proofs.
2. faith or trust.
3. a religious tenet or tenets.
4. *Biblical:* a trusting relationship with God.
5. *Personal:* a life-changing confidence that God does what he promises to do.

Believing is Seeing

Jesus said . . . "I am the resurrection and
the life; he who believes in Me will live
even if he dies, and everyone who lives
and believes in Me will never die."

John 11: 25–26 NASB

How do you please God? First and foremost, you please him by believing that what he says is true. You become a child of God through belief. God makes his promises real in your life through belief. But what if you only believe a little bit, or what if you're troubled by doubts? How much belief does it take for God to work in your life?

The apostle Mark told of a father who came to Jesus with his demon-possessed son. The disciples had been unable to help, and the man had doubts that Jesus could do anything either. But the man was desperate. "If you can do anything," he begged, "take pity on us and help us!" Jesus answered, "All things are possible to him who believes." "I do believe," the man replied. "Help me in my unbelief."

words
to live by

This sounds a little confused, doesn't it? The man said he believed, and then he asked Jesus to help him in his unbelief. But even in his unbelief, he got it right. In Jesus the man saw not only the One he could believe in, but the One who could give him the will to believe more perfectly. This desperate father didn't place his trust in his own ability to believe. He placed his trust in the Christ who could set his son free. And his son was delivered. In response to the father's shaky but honest faith, Jesus performed a miracle and cast the demon out.

> Belief is not mainly an agreement with facts in the head; it is mainly an appetite in the heart which fastens on Jesus for satisfaction.
> **JOHN PIPER**

Do you ever feel that you don't believe enough? Does your spiritual life feel like a continual struggle to muster up more belief? There's good news for you: Your status before God depends on God's faithfulness, not yours. Belief the size of a mustard seed is enough to move mountains—as long as that belief rests in the God who is able to move mountains. Sure, your belief will waver. You're a human being, after all. You'll experience doubts. But the God who began a good work in you is faithful to complete it.

Belief is a little bit like sitting in a chair. Putting your weight into a chair requires a certain amount of trust. You have to believe the chair is strong enough to hold you up. If you didn't believe that, you'd continue standing (or maybe you'd find another chair to put your trust in). But once you sit down, what is it that keeps you from falling to the ground? It's not the strength of your belief; it's the strength of the chair. In the same

dness grace mercy love faith goodness truth freedom hope
forgiveness peace humble holiness obey repent perfect submit
serve fellowship comforter transformed noble character church

way, Jesus' grace and power uphold and sustain you when you place your trust in him, even when your faith is weak.

How much do you have to believe before God can work in your life? You have to believe enough to rest your whole weight on him. God is faithful, strong to save, and more than able to support you. You don't have to have everything figured out. God accepts even the smallest, weakest act of belief. But he won't let your belief stay small and weak. God rewards belief by giving even greater belief. You've heard people say, "I'll believe it when I see it." Jesus turns that around. When it comes to the promises of God, you believe first, and then you see. In the meantime, it's enough to say, like the father who brought his son to Jesus, "I do believe; help me in my unbelief."

> Abram believed the
> LORD, and the LORD
> declared him righteous
> because of his faith.
> **Genesis 15:6 NLT**

do something

Keep a "promise journal." As you read your Bible, watch for God's promises to his people, and record them in a notebook. On the left-hand page, write down the scriptural promise. On the right-hand page, write down ways you've seen that promise fulfilled. At first it may be hard to think of real-life examples of promises fulfilled. But just wait: As you focus on God's faithfulness, you'll soon run out of room on the right-hand page.

words
to live by

What if some did not believe? Will their unbelief make the faithfulness of God without effect?
Romans 3:3 NKJV

If we only have the will to walk, then God is pleased with our stumbles.
C. S. LEWIS

The Tannese islanders had no word meaning *belief*. But when missionary John Paton saw an islander resting in a chair, he translated *believe*, using the Tannese word meaning "rest your whole weight upon"—their word for sitting in a chair.

The word *believe* is related to the Old English word *lEof*, which comes down to us as the word *love*. Ultimately, the things you believe in are the things you love or hold dear.

final thought

God, once I stepped out in faith, I realized that you are more trustworthy than I had ever imagined. Thank you. Amen.

Believing Is Seeing

bless·ing, verb

1. the act of one that blesses.
2. a short prayer said before or after a meal; grace.
3. something promoting or contributing to happiness, well-being, or prosperity; a boon.
4. approbation; approval: *This plan has my blessing.*
5. **Biblical:** words spoken to make holy; gifts, either spiritual or material, given by God.
6. **Personal:** God's good intentions toward us.

From Happiness to Greater Happiness

Let GOD bless all who fear GOD—bless
the small, bless the great.
Psalm 115:13 THE MESSAGE

Two people are riding down the highway in a car. In front of them, a truck blows a tire and careens across three lanes of traffic. The car is headed straight toward the swerving truck. From the look of things, there's no avoiding a terrible crash. The car's driver stands on the brake pedal and whips the steering wheel. A blur of trees and truck and pavement spins past, and the passengers' lives flash before their eyes. One rotation. Two rotations. And then, as suddenly as it began, it's over. The car comes to a stop. The truck driver regains control.

Hearts pounding, the car's passengers look back at the still-smoking trails of black rubber left on the pavement. Their own looping skid marks come within inches of the thick black marks left by the truck. But everyone is unscathed. Driver and passenger stare slack-jawed and speak simultaneously.

words
to live by

"Whew," says the driver. "What a piece of luck!"

"Whew," says the passenger. "What a blessing!"

What's the difference between good luck and a blessing? When you refer to a bit of good fortune as a "blessing," you're acknowledging that it came from God. It's not just a random bit of happiness that happened to fall in your lap, but rather it's another bit of evidence confirming the truth that God is always working things out to the good of his people.

> Lift up your eyes. The heavenly Father waits to bless you in inconceivable ways to make your life what you never dreamed it could be.
> **ANNE ORTLUND**

A blessing isn't ultimately about you. It's about your fulfilling the purposes that God has for you. Yes, a blessing brings you happiness. But the real point is that it equips you for the deeper happiness of fulfilling God's purpose for your life. To say "I feel lucky" is to say "In the random distribution of good feelings and bad feelings, I've been getting more than my share of good feelings lately." To say "I feel blessed" is to wonder "How is this God-sent happiness going to lead me and those around me to greater happiness?" It's to ask "Why did God just rescue me from danger?" or "Why did God give me all these material things?"

What are you doing when you "ask a blessing" before a meal? First, you are acknowledging that this food, like all other good gifts, comes from God. And second, you're asking that God's purposes for that food—your nourishment, your enjoyment—be fulfilled. In essence, you are saying to God, "Take this food that you have given me, and use it to do your work." That's what it means for food to be blessed. It's not ultimately about the food, but rather your good and God's glory.

> Praise the God and Father of our Lord Jesus Christ! Through Christ, God has blessed us with every spiritual blessing that heaven has to offer.
>
> **Ephesians 1:3** GOD'S WORD

Have that same attitude when you ask God's blessing on your own life. Don't pray, "God, send a little luck my way." Rather, pray, "God, give me your good gifts, so that your blessings in my life might overflow into the lives of those around me, and so that I might move toward completeness in Christ."

do something

God blessed Abraham so that he might be a blessing to others—not just so that Abraham would experience happiness, but so that many others might experience the same happiness of knowing the God who works in the lives of human beings. Think about the ways in which God has blessed you most richly. How might those blessings overflow into other people's lives?

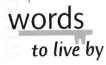

words
to live by

Reflect on your present blessings, of which every man has many; not on your past misfortunes, of which all men have some.
CHARLES DICKENS

It is the blessing of the LORD that makes rich, and He adds no sorrow to it.
Proverbs 10:22 NASB

The word *bless* in all its forms appears 472 times in the Bible. *Blessing* is truly the work of God.

In the ancient world, a beatitude could be used as a form of compliment or congratulation: "Blessed are you, teacher, who are so wise." But Jesus took that familiar form and turned it on its head. "Blessed are you when men cast insults at you." That's pretty radical.

final thought

God, thank you for showing me that the deepest blessing is the confidence that you mean to do me good—and that you always finish what you set out to do. Amen.

ones, grace mercy love faith goodness gentleness
godliness peace humble holiness obey repent perfect submit
erve fellowship comforter transformed noble character church

choice, noun

1. an act of selecting freely and after consideration.
2. the opportunity to choose.
3. an inclination toward.
4. **Biblical:** something desired or preferred.
5. **Personal:** the pursuit of one's desires.

You Want?

If serving the Lord seems undesirable
to you, then choose for yourselves
this day whom you will serve. . . .
But as for me and my household,
we will serve the LORD.

Joshua 24:15 NIV

Your life is a series of choices. You make hundreds of choices every day—what to wear, what to say, how to act, what to think about. Every choice you make comes down to a single question: What do you want? When faced with two options, you always choose the one you want most. Sometimes, of course, you find yourself in situations where all the options seem lousy. You don't exactly want to give your lunch money to the class bully, but getting beaten up is something you want even less. So you choose to fork it over.

It seems simple enough, but here's where it gets complicated: You're a tangle of conflicting desires. You want to make good grades, but you also like playing video games. You want to be healthy, but junk food sure does taste good. You want to please God, but you also want to please your friends. Whenever you are

words
to live by

faced with a choice, either conscious or unconscious, you choose that which you desire most *at the moment of decision*. That's the key: *at the moment of decision.* Human desires are in constant conflict, and they constantly fluctuate. You don't always want the same thing, so you don't always choose the same thing.

Think about your choice to get out of bed this morning. Unless somebody physically dragged you out of bed, you made a choice to get up. If you're like most people, you probably don't get out of bed the second you wake up. The alarm goes off, and you reach over and hit the snooze button. At that moment, no desire over-matches your desire to stay in that nice, comfortable bed. But at some point this morning some other desire overcame your desire for rest. Maybe you remembered you had a test today, so you jumped up to cram a few extra minutes before school. Maybe your little brother was jumping on your bed and singing at the top of his lungs. Your desire to put an end to that won out easily over all other desires.

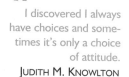

I discovered I always have choices and some-times it's only a choice of attitude.

JUDITH M. KNOWLTON

That may seem a trivial example, but it illustrates two important truths about every choice you make. First, your wants are in conflict with each other. You want your rest, you want to study for important tests, and you want to avoid being annoyed by bed-jumping siblings. When those desires come into conflict, you have to choose between them. Second, those wants move up and down in relative importance. At five in the morning, the desire for sleep is stronger than the desire to

ones grace mercy ... good ... freedom hope
rgiveness peace humble holiness obey repent perfect submit
ive fellowship comforter transformed noble character church

study. At six-thirty, the desire to study may be stronger.

Choosing the right things means wanting the right things. You want to please God. That's good. But living a holy life—choosing right instead of wrong—requires not just that you want to please God, but that you want to please God more than you want to sin at the moment you're forced to choose. The desire for God isn't something you conjure up only in those moments of moral crisis. It's cultivated over time, developed in the quiet moments when you're not in the heat of spiritual battle. Strengthen your desire to know God, to please God, and when you're faced with a choice, you'll choose what's right.

> It was by faith that Moses, when he grew up, refused to be treated as the son of Pharaoh's daughter. He chose to share the oppression of God's people instead of enjoying the fleeting pleasures of sin.
> **Hebrews 11:24–25** NLT

do something

What do you want? Everybody wants lots of different things, contradictory things. But what is it that you really want? A bad choice is simply letting a lesser want—or a temporary, impulsive want—get in the way of what you truly want for your life. Don't let yourself lose sight of the things that you want the most.

words
to live by

I have set before you life and death, blessing and cursing; therefore choose life, that both you and your descendants may live.

Deuteronomy 30:19
NKJV

One definition of *maturity* is the ability to make short-term choices that match up with your long-term goals. It's also called the principle of delayed gratification.

Research shows that people work best—whether at school or in a business environment—when they feel that they have been able to choose their work.

Every time you make a choice you are turning the central part of you, the part of you that chooses, into something a little different from what it was before.

C. S. LEWIS

final thought

God, I am at a time in my life when I'm faced with more choices than ever before. Give me wisdom to choose well. Give me a heart that wants what's right at the moment of choice. Amen.

church, noun

1. a building for public and especially Christian worship.
2. a body or organization of religious believers.
3. a: the whole body of Christians; b: denomination; c: congregation.
4. **Biblical:** the Christian community, either locally or universally; the gathering of believers.
5. **Personal:** the body of Christ on earth, made up of believing Christians.

Where Does God Live?

Present yourselves as building stones for the construction of a sanctuary vibrant with life, in which you'll serve as holy priests offering Christ-approved lives up to God.

1 Peter 2:5 THE MESSAGE

The Old Testament temple in Jerusalem was an awesome place. Built on the highest hill in the city, it was as tall as a seventeen-story building—an architectural marvel for its time. Each of its twelve gates was as high as a three-story building, just as wide, and covered in gold. Its massive pillars were made of marble and gold. Its embroidered tapestries demonstrated incredible artistry and years of painstaking labor. The sweet smell of incense and the beautiful music of worship filled the air around the temple hill. Joyous praise, solemn repentance, the whole range of emotion for the people of God found their deepest expression there in God's dwelling place on earth.

If ever a building shone forth the glory of God, it was the temple in Jerusalem. Here was the beauty of God, the immensity of God, the power of God reflected for everyone to see. The very

words
to live by

sight of it made the righteous glad. And even the heathen who came to Jerusalem saw in the temple a glimpse of the God who made them and who still had a claim on them.

But the most amazing thing about the temple is the fact that it was only a foreshadowing of God's true dwelling on earth: the Church. God doesn't dwell in a building—not even a building as impressive as the Jerusalem temple. No, the dwelling place of God on earth is the people who make up the Church. You are one of the stones of God's house, and Christ is the Cornerstone. The glory of that house overshadows even the temple's glory.

> The Church is a society of sinners—the only society in the world in which membership is based upon the single qualification that the candidate shall be unworthy of membership.
>
> **CHARLES C. MORRISON**

It seems hard to believe, doesn't it? You might not feel like you're showing forth the glory of God. But it's right there in the Scriptures: Through his Church, God displays the rich variety of his wisdom, not merely to the world, but even to the angels who eagerly watch to see what the people of God are going to do next (Ephesians 3:10). Looking around on Sunday morning, you may wonder how God could possibly use that crowd to display his majesty and wisdom to a watching world. They're just regular people. Some of them are your classmates. Some are people like your parents. Some are little kids who fall asleep during the sermon. But that's the way God works. He uses the regular guys just as much as he uses the superstars.

It's easy to get discouraged by church—when the leadership seems out of touch, when your peers in youth group seem as worldly as everybody else, when Sunday services seem dry and irrelevant to the rest of your life. But that doesn't change the fact that the Church is God's dwelling place on earth. It is through the Church that God is going to work out his great and glorious plan for the world. No wonder the writer of Hebrews warns us not to give up the habit of meeting together. We're here to love one another, to be not just the home of Christ, but the very Body of Christ in the world he came to redeem. This is serious business.

> Let us not give up the habit of meeting together, as some are doing. Instead, let us encourage one another all the more, since you see that the Day of the Lord is coming nearer.
> **Hebrews 10:25** GNT

do something

God is able to show forth his glory and wisdom any way he chooses. But the main way he chooses to show his glory—the main way he demonstrates what kind of God he is—is through his people. You are a stone of Christ's dwelling on earth. You're still a little rough, and you won't be perfectly squared off this side of heaven, but you and your fellow believers make up God's temple.

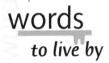
words
to live by

Christ is the head of
the church, which is
his body.
Colossians 1:18 NLT

Thank God, a seven-
year-old child knows
what the church is,
namely, holy believers
and sheep who hear the
voice of their Shepherd.
MARTIN LUTHER

🏹 If you want to see serious
church growth, look at Africa. In
1900, there were about 10 million
Christians in Africa, about 9% of
the population. In 2000, there
were 360 million African
Christians, about 46% of the population.

🏹 Bible teachers distinguish
between the "visible church" and
the "invisible church." The visible
church consists of everyone who
professes Christ—everyone who
looks like a Christian. But only
God can see into the heart; only
God knows who has been reborn.
Those people constitute the true
Church, the invisible church.

final thought

God, I am amazed that you would choose to display your glory on
earth through people like me. Help me to love my fellow
Christians—your Church. Cement us together, with Christ as our
cornerstone. May we be a suitable dwelling for you. Amen.

com·fort, noun

1. strengthening aid.
2. consolation in time of trouble or worry; solace.
3. a feeling of relief or encouragement.
4. **Biblical:** assistance in a time of need; literally, a calling to one's side.
5. **Personal:** a healing touch on a life that has been broken.

Who'd Have Guessed It?

Blessed are those who mourn.
They will be comforted.
Matthew 5:4 GOD'S WORD

Do you ever feel broken? The sting of a bad grade, the hurt of a breakup, the sorrow of losing a loved one all give you the feeling that this isn't what you were made for. And indeed you weren't made for the disappointments and losses of a life lived in this fallen world. You were made for heaven, where every tear will be wiped away. But in the meantime, God gives his comfort, a little taste of the eternal rest of heaven.

God delights to bring good things out of bad, to rescue what appear to be impossible cases. Think of Joseph, betrayed by his brothers, falsely accused, languishing in prison. What sorrow, what disappointment and discouragement must he have felt? God redeemed that situation and through it saved the Hebrew people. Looking back, Joseph was able to say to his brothers, "What you meant for evil, God meant for good." But in the midst of his

words
to live by

sorrow, when he couldn't yet see how things would work out, he had to walk by faith, not by sight. God was right there at his side even in his deepest need.

Or consider the deep, soul-wrenching sorrow of Christ's disciples in the days after Jesus was crucified. How could they understand that this was God's plan all along? But even when they thought God had abandoned them, he was at work. From the sadness, the shame, the apparent meaninglessness of an innocent man being tortured to death, God worked the salvation of his Church. The world's deepest sorrow became the world's richest joy when God snatched life out of the jaws of death.

> Even in the winter, even in the midst of the storm, the sun is still there. Somewhere, up above the clouds, it still shines and warms and pulls at the life buried deep inside the brown branches and frozen earth.
>
> GLORIA GAITHER

That's how God always works. He turns your reality inside out, lest you should ever think you've got it figured out and don't need God. He causes the last to become the first. He uses the weak to shame the strong, the foolish to shame the wise. And those who mourn will be happy. From an earthly perspective, who'd have guessed it?

Are you sorrowful, in need of comfort? Remember, you don't know the whole story. You're a human being. No human being knows the whole story. But God does. And even if you don't know every detail, you do know how the story ends.

comfort · comfort · comfort · comfort · comfort

Everything works for the good of God's people. The question, then, is never "I wonder whether this is going to turn out okay," but rather, "I wonder how this is going to turn out okay." You aren't the victim of circumstances beyond God's control.

God is your comfort. As Joni Earickson Tada said, in the end, it's not an answer you need, but a person. That's why God gives himself, in the form of his Spirit, the Great Comforter, who comes alongside us in times of need.

> You can be sure that the more we suffer for Christ, the more God will shower us with his comfort through Christ.
> **2 Corinthians 1:5** NLT

Take comfort in the fact that God will work everything out for your good and his glory. That's your future hope. But for the present, know that even now God is with you. He hasn't forgotten you.

do something

When you're hurting and in need of comfort, share your need with other Christians. It will serve two purposes: First, God often uses other Christians to help heal hurts. And second, your sharing may be a ministry to a Christian brother or sister. By making yourself vulnerable to other believers, by giving others a chance to minister to you, you open the door to genuine fellowship.

words
to live by

Let not your heart be troubled; you believe in God, believe also in Me.
John 14:1 NKJV

God does not comfort us to make us comfortable, but to make us comforters.
JOHN HENRY JOWETT

⫟ One of the names for the Holy Spirit is "the Comforter" (sometimes translated "the Helper" or "the Advocate"). Jesus refered to the Spirit as *parakletos*, One who is called to a person's side to help or comfort. In 1 John 2:1, John refered to Jesus using the same term.

⫟ The Jews who looked forward to the coming of the Messiah often spoke of that great day as "the Comfort (or Consolation) of Israel." Christ came to be comfort to those who are hurting.

Final thought

God, thank you that none of my hurts is too small to bring before you. No sorrow is beyond your comfort. No loneliness can keep you from coming to my side. No darkness can keep your light from streaming through. Amen.

com·mun·ion, *noun*

com·mun·ion · com·mun·ion

1. an act or instance of sharing.
2. (cap.) a Christian sacrament in which consecrated bread and wine are consumed as memorials of Christ's death.
3. intimate fellowship or rapport; communication.
4. *Biblical:* fellowship with God and with other Christians; the union of all Christian believers.
5. *Personal:* a deep connection with God.

If we live in the light in the same way that God is in the light, we have a relationship with each other. And the blood of his Son Jesus cleanses us from every sin.

1 John 1:7 GOD'S WORD

Do you ever go out for pizza with your friends after church or youth group? Kicking back with your friends and enjoying a meal together after the "official" church activities are over can be a major highlight. There might even be people in your youth group who consider after-church pizza to be the main attraction. That attitude may not be as unspiritual as it sounds. Communing with other Christians over a shared meal has a very long history.

The earliest Christians didn't go out to eat together after their church service. They went out to eat together *during* the service. They gathered around tables and ate together before the preaching and hymn-singing started. They called it the "love feast," and it wasn't just a symbolic meal. It was a real meal, where they sat down hungry and got up full. For the poorer members of

words
to live by

the congregation, it might be the biggest meal they had all week, made possible by the more well-off members of the congregation. No doubt it was a time of fun and fellowship, as meals shared between friends always are. As those early Christians communed with God, they grew closer to one another.

What do you think of when you hear the word *communion*?

You probably think of a symbolic mini-meal consisting of a tiny piece of bread and a sip of grape juice or wine. The Communion ceremony, or the Lord's Supper, represents the Christian's union with God. It's one of the most important rituals of the Christian faith. It's a concrete reminder that you have a hunger that can only be satisfied by God—and that God became a man and allowed his body to be broken and his blood spilled so that this hunger might be satisfied. God spreads a feast for you, and that feast is himself.

The idea of Communion goes well beyond the Lord's Supper, however. Communion is a deep communication or connection with God. He invites you to feed on him, to chew on his Word and be satisfied, not just when you "take Communion," but every day. In some respects, Communion with God looks more like a pizza than the bread and cup of the Lord's Supper. It's not an occasional meal; rather, it's standard, everyday fare for a Christian. It's rich and filling.

ndness grace mercy love faith goodness truth freedom hope
orgiveness peace humble holiness obey repent perfect submit
erve fellowship comforter transformed noble character church

Communion with God always results in communion with other believers who also commune with him. That's why the early Christians' love feasts, in combination with the Lord's Supper, provide a more complete picture of Communion than the Lord's Supper by itself. When early Christian congregations sat down to eat before the service, they were feasting together literally, not just symbolically. The act of sharing a meal—enjoying the same tastes and smells, laughing and joking, passing the salt—served to cement their love for one another. To commune with Christ is to join a feast with other Christians. Pull up a chair.

Taste and see that the LORD is good.
Psalm 34:8 NLT

do something

God promises that everyone who hungers and thirsts for righteousness will be filled. This is one hunger that you can be sure will be satisfied—not meagerly, but richly. God prepares a feast for everyone who wishes to commune with him, like a deep-dish special. And it's usually shared elbow-to-elbow with friends and family.

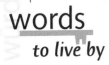

words
to live by

The goal is for all of them to become one heart and mind—just as you, Father, are in me and I in you, so they might be one heart and mind with us. Then the world might believe that you, in fact, sent me.
John 17:21 THE MESSAGE

A habit of devout fellowship with God is the spring of all our life, and the strength of it.
HENRY EDWARD MANNING

Ever wonder what you'll be doing in heaven? For one thing, you'll be sitting down to a feast with the other residents of heaven—the Marriage Supper of the Lamb (see Revelation 19:7–9). Any time you share a meal with fellow believers, think of it as practice.

The first deacons in the Church were waiters at the love feasts. The apostle Paul instituted the office of deacon to help out the elders, who were spending so much time and effort serving at the love feasts that they had insufficient time for their teaching and preaching duties.

final thought

God, you invite me to feed on you and be made full, but I don't always feel hungry. Make me hunger for you, God, that I might be filled. Amen.

God's Table

con·tent·ment, noun

1. the quality or state of having one's desires appeased.
2. pleasure or pleasurable satisfaction.
3. *Biblical:* the sense of assurance that God provides all needs.
4. *Personal:* the ability to want what one already has.

Contain Yourself

Now godliness with contentment is great gain.
I Timothy 6:6 NKJV

The little boy is standing in his seat. He can't contain his excitement. He stuffs his mouth with cotton candy. He sips a frozen lemonade. The other seats are filling up. The circus will start any minute now. The arena goes completely dark, leaving only the green exit signs visible. Suddenly the white shaft of a spotlight pierces the blackness and illuminates the tall figure of a man in a shiny black top hat and a red tail coat. "Ladies and gentlemen," he intones into his microphone, "children of all ages." The little boy is in heaven. The elephants! The clowns! The dancing ponies! The tightrope walkers! He's been begging to go to the circus, and now that he's here, it's more marvelous than he could have imagined.

The boy sits transfixed, drinking in everything that happens in all three rings. His enraptured silence is broken only by the occasional squeal of delight. Then he glimpses a flash of color in the darkened aisle beside him. It's a vendor selling plastic light-up

words
to live by

swords. The boy notices for the first time that other children throughout the arena are waving swords just like them, making hundreds of little rainbows in the darkened seats. He points at the vendor and turns to his parents.

"I want one."

"No, son" his father answers, "You don't need that. You've got lots of swords at home."

"But I want one!" the boy says a little more loudly.

"No, darling." It's his mother this time. "We're not buying anything else. Oh, look, honey. Acrobats!"

> Faith in God will not get for you everything you want, but it will get for you what God wants you to have. The unbeliever does not need what he wants; the Christian should want only what he needs.
> **VANCE HAVNER**

But by now the little boy is on his way to a full-blown tantrum. "I want one! I want one! I want one!" He's bent over the back of his seat, reaching for the sword vendor. He makes such a scene his father has to carry him out in disgrace.

That's a picture of discontentment. When the little boy turned his attention to what he didn't have, he could no longer enjoy what he did have. He was having the time of his life until it occurred to him that others might be having the time of their lives *and* getting light-up swords on top of it. Contentment is just the opposite: It's the ability to be satisfied with what God has given you, whether it's a lot or a little.

People usually talk about contentment in the context of material things. Contentment is being satisfied with driving an old clunker because it beats having to walk. Or being happy to walk, because the exercise and fresh air are good for you. Discontentment, by contrast, is being mad that your parents only bought you a BMW, when your friend's parents bought him a Porsche.

But contentment and discontentment apply to more than material things. Are you content with the abilities that God has given you? Are you satisfied with your place in the pecking order at school? Are you always striving to be someone you're not? God always gives you everything you need, even if it's not everything you think you want. He will put you where you need to be. Trust him. And don't make yourself miserable by dwelling on what God has chosen not to give you.

> Those who love money will never have enough. How absurd to think that wealth brings true happiness!
> **Ecclesiastes 5:10** NLT

do something

Nothing neutralizes your happiness more quickly than discontentment with what you've been given. One of the first signs of discontentment is the feeling that you deserve something you don't have. When you feel discontentment creeping into your life, turn your attention away from what you "deserve" and toward the good things that God has blessed you with already.

words
to live by

The cheerful heart has a continual feast. Better a little with the fear of the LORD than great wealth with turmoil.
Proverbs 15:15–16 NIV

When Christ reveals Himself there is satisfaction in the slenderest portion, and without Christ there is emptiness in the greatest fullness.
ALEXANDER GROSSE

Do you ever feel you'd be content if you just had a little more money, or a few more things? The United Nations' 2002 Human Development Report might put things in perspective. The average American income is five times that of the average income for the rest of the world.

The word *contentment* comes from the same root as the word *contained*. To be content is to keep your wants and desires contained within the limits of what you have.

final thought

God, you are the Giver of good gifts. You never fail to give me what I need. Rescue me from the bitterness and unhappiness that come from the mistaken belief that you have given me less than I deserve. Make me content with the blessings you have showered on me. Amen.

Contain Yourself

cour·age, noun

1. the mental or moral strength to venture, persevere, and withstand danger, fear, or difficulty.
2. fearlessness, bravery, valor.
3. to act in accordance with one's beliefs, especially in the face of criticism; to have the courage of one's convictions.
4. **Biblical:** the confidence or freedom from fear that comes from a trust in God.
5. **Personal:** the ability, in times of hardship, danger, or difficulty, to ignore natural fear and pursue one's convictions.

the Land

Don't be afraid, for I am with you. Do not be dismayed, for I am your God. I will strengthen you. I will help you. I will uphold you with my victorious right hand.
Isaiah 41:10 NLT

When the twelve spies reported back to the Israelites after checking out the Promised Land for the first time, they offered a classic good news / bad news scenario. Yes, they reported, God was right about one thing: It was truly a land flowing with milk and honey. But God hadn't mentioned the fact that there were giants in the land. They weren't the sort of people who would be easily persuaded to leave, no matter what Moses said about Canaan being the Israelites' inheritance.

So ten of the twelve spies did the natural thing: They lost hope. "We can't attack those people," they said. "They are stronger than we are. . . . We seemed like grasshoppers in our own eyes, and we looked the same to them" (Numbers 13:31, 33 NIV). There were two spies, however, who were able to look beyond the natural world and see their situation in the light of God's

words
to live by

presence. Joshua and Caleb managed to remember, in the face of such frightening opposition, that it had always been God who fought for them and that God was faithful to keep his promise. Joshua and Caleb simply remembered what God had said and what God had done.

The people of Israel refused to remember. Rather than showing courage, they gave in to the fear of the ten spies. They looked at the earthly facts of the matter—big Canaanites, little Israelites—and forgot about the greater fact of God's

It is only the fear of God that can deliver us from the fear of man.
JOHN WITHERSPOON.

protection. For the people of God, fear is a kind of forgetfulness. It robs you of happiness that is yours for the taking (the fearful Israelites, you may remember, missed out on their chance to enter the Promised Land). And it's an insult to the God who promises you something better than a fear-limited life. Consider God's response when the people of Israel chose fear instead of courage: "How long will these people treat me like dirt? How long refuse to trust me? And with all these signs I've done among them!" (Numbers 14:11 THE MESSAGE).

The irony of fear is that even as it distorts your ability to see what's really true, it convinces you that you're just being realistic. The ten spies thought they were the ones who were being realistic and that Joshua and Caleb were just wild-eyed dreamers. "Get a grip," you can see them saying. "Look at the facts, will you?" But the more they looked at the "facts," the less they were able to keep things in perspective. Soon a challenging situation began to look like an impossible situation, and the ten spies shrank into their own fears: "We seemed like grasshoppers in our own eyes." Who's being unrealistic now?

What giants do you face? What are the situations that keep you from going forward boldly, courageously to claim the abundant life that Christ promised? Perhaps you fear the disapproval of your schoolmates. Maybe you have a teacher whose intimidating manner keeps you from expressing your true opinions in class. Perhaps you have fears about the future—college, career, family. The world can be a frightening place. But God has promised that he will provide your every need, heal your every hurt, calm your every fear. God is with his people.

> Only be strong and very courageous.
> Joshua 1:7 NASB

And if God is with you, who can stand against you?

do something

For a Christian, courage isn't the same thing as self-confidence. Rather, it's a confidence in God. It's the ability to remember, in spite of the fears and challenges of life, that God always shows himself strong on behalf of his people.

words
to live by

"Behold, the virgin shall be with child, and bear a Son, and they shall call His name Immanuel," which is translated, "God with us."
Matthew 1:23 NKJV

Courage is not simply one of the virtues, but the form of every virtue at the testing point, which means, at the point of highest reality. A chastity or honesty or mercy which yields to danger will be chaste or honest or merciful only on conditions. Pilate was merciful until it became risky.
C. S. Lewis

⟁ Who, exactly, were the ten Israelite spies afraid of? One especially frightening character was Og, King of Bashan. This Canaanite chieftain slept in an iron bed that was thirteen feet long and six feet wide.

⟁ Waorani tribesmen in the Amazon jungle murdered five missionaries. Two of the missionaries' wives, Elisabeth Eliot and Rachel Saint, returned to the scene of the crime to continue their husbands' work. The love and forgiveness showed by those women so amazed the Waorani that they received the gospel message.

Final thought

God, sometimes I forget that you are always with me. My courage fails because I too often look at my situation with the eyes of the world, and not the eyes of faith. Give me the courage that comes from remembering who you are and what you have promised to me. Amen.

Giants in the Land

cov·e·nant, noun

1. a usually formal, solemn, and binding agreement.
2. a written promise between two or more parties especially for the performance of some action.
3. a common-law action to recover damages for breach of promise.
4. **Biblical:** an arrangement or agreement between two parties, especially between God and his people.
5. **Personal:** the promise by which God binds himself to give his blessings to his people.

God's Contract

I will not leave you until I have
done what I have promised you.
Genesis 28:15 NIV

When you buy a car someday, you might sign a loan contract. By the terms of that agreement, the bank agrees to give you enough money to buy the car, and you agree to pay the money back on a monthly schedule. In signing that paper, you're also agreeing to a serious penalty if you fail to keep your end of the bargain: You'll lose the car. That's the way contracts work; both sides agree to do certain things for the other, but they also agree to accept certain penalties if they don't meet their commitments.

The people of the ancient world had binding contracts too, though they weren't always signed pieces of paper. One of the most well-known rituals for formalizing an agreement was called the cutting of a covenant. If two kings were entering into a treaty, they might kill one or more animals, cut them in two, and spread the pieces on the ground. Then one or both of the kings would

words
to live by

walk between the pieces. It was a way of saying, "If I do not abide by this agreement, may I be cut to pieces just as these animals have been." If the agreement was between kings of roughly equal strength, both would usually walk between the pieces. Sometimes, if one king was significantly stronger than the other, only the weaker king would walk between the pieces. It was only the weaker king, after all, who was in serious danger of being cut to pieces if he broke the treaty.

> If God be your God, and Christ your Christ, the Lord has a special, peculiar favour to you; you are the object of His choice, accepted in His beloved Son.
> **CHARLES SPURGEON**

The Bible describes the relationship between God and his people as a covenant that began with Abram and continues even now. God promised Abram that he would make a great nation of his descendants. To seal the agreement, God and Abraham cut a covenant. But the astonishing thing about this covenant-cutting was that God, not Abraham, passed between the pieces of the sacrifice. It was God, the infinitely stronger King, who took upon himself the penalties implied in the covenant. God wasn't binding Abram to the covenant, he was binding himself.

That same covenant applies to you. If you are in Christ, God has bound himself to you, to make you part of that great nation of Abraham's descendants. You cannot earn your place in that covenant, nor can you un-earn it. God, not you, has taken that responsibility. Within that big covenant, however, there are smaller covenants; in these, you do have responsibil-

ness grace mercy love faith goodness truth freedom hope
giveness peace humble holiness obey repent perfect submit
ve fellowship comforter transformed noble character church

ities. The Ten Commandments are a kind of covenant. On the basis of those commandments, God promises to reward righteousness and to punish wrongdoing. If you choose to disobey, you miss out on the rewards of obedience. But you will not, cannot lose your place in the larger covenant. You belong to God forever; God has sworn by himself.

It's as if the bank president presented you with a contract that read, "We, the bank, will provide you with the money you need to buy your dream car. But should you fail to hold up your end of the bargain, we will assume all the penalties resulting from that failure." That's the kind of God you serve. This is the Covenant: not that you have anything to bring to God, but that he chose to bring himself to you. He took the penalties inherent in the Covenant—the death, the brokenness—on himself, so that you might live, so that you might be whole.

> I will not dishonor my promise or alter my own agreement. On my holiness I have taken an oath once and for all: I will not lie to David.
> **Psalm 89:34–35**
> GOD'S WORD

do something

God does not lie. People break contracts all the time. But God will not break his Covenant with his people, no matter what. God has bound himself to an agreement in which we receive all the benefits and he takes on all the penalties. What a Gospel.

words
to live by

Remember that the LORD your God is the only God and that he is faithful. He will keep his covenant and show his constant love to a thousand generations of those who love him and obey his commands.
Deuteronomy 7:9 GNT

The words of human beings are unstable things. But not so the words of God. They stand forever, as abidingly valid expressions of his mind and thought.
J. I. PACKER

▼ *Berit*, the Hebrew word translated *covenant*, literally means "fetter" or "bond." When God entered into a covenant with you, it's as if he handcuffed himself to you.

▼ The oldest known written contracts, or covenants, came from Mesopotamia, perhaps from the time period when Abraham lived there. Anthropologists believe that cuneiform, the earliest form of writing, developed as the result of Sumerians' need to write out sales contracts.

final thought

God, not only have you chosen to offer me the benefits of a covenant relationship, you have also chosen to take the penalties of that covenant on yourself. I adore and thank you with all the love my human heart can muster. Amen.

ofless grace mercy love faith doctrine truth freedom hope
orgiveness peace humble holiness obey repent perfect submit
erve fellowship comforter transformed noble character church

cre·a·tion, noun

1. the act of producing or causing to exist.
2. the original bringing into existence of the world.
3. a thing that has been created.
4. **Biblical:** God's act of making an entire universe out of pure nothingness.
5. **Personal:** God's artistry in the natural world.

The Mirror of God's Glory

The heavens declare the glory of God, and the sky displays what his hands have made. One day tells a story to the next. One night shares knowledge with the next.

Psalm 19:1–2 GOD'S WORD

Standing at the base of a big waterfall is an almost over-whelming experience. The foaming water plunges down the rock face and into the swirling pool below with a never-ceasing thunder that seems to speak of the awesome power of God. The leaves of the mountain laurel, wet with spray, nod and bow in the constantly shifting breeze kicked up by the collision of water on water. And when the sun slants down just right, you can see the arch of a rainbow suspended in the mist over the emerald pool.

A flower is no less awe-inspiring, if you look closely enough. The incredible intricacies of its design, its fragile balance, its symmetry all speak of a Designer who has an eye for microscopic detail—a Designer who cares about the little things. Its delicate beauty and its vibrant color speak of a Creator who goes beyond

words
to live by

the merely useful and necessary and fills his creation with delight after delight.

Or consider the stars on a moonless night, when you're far from the lights of town. Thousands upon thousands of twinkling lights shimmer against the black backdrop of the sky, the nearest star millions of miles away, every one as brilliant as the sun, every single star in its place. And the part you can see is just one tiny corner of the universe. It blew Isaiah's mind to think of it: "Look up at the sky! Who created the stars you see? The one who leads them out like an army, he knows how many there are and calls each one by name! His power is so great—not one of them is ever missing!" (Isaiah 40:26 GNT).

> Consider the beauty and fragrance of the flowers, the exquisite nature of the butterfly, the stateliness of the horse, the cuddliness of the little puppy. Look up at the stars in their courses and at the sun sending forth its life-giving rays. In all the works of nature let your mind dwell upon the glorious wisdom of God.
>
> JERRY BRIDGES

When you let your imagination be captured by the wonders of such a world, you can't help but wonder: If the creation is this incredible, what must the Creator be like? And you can only marvel that such a Creator, who crafts every flower, cares about your every need. This Creator, who sets every star in place, knows every hair that falls from your head. This Creator loved you so much that he gave his only Son for you.

Here's one of the most amazing things about the creation:

ness grace mercy love faith goodness grant freedom hope
forgiveness peace humble holiness obey repent perfect submit
serve fellowship comforter transformed noble character church

the crowning work of the natural order, the pinnacle of God's handiwork, is you. Of all the marvels of creation, you are the most marvelous. For you are made in the image of God. Your mind, your creativity, your ability to love, your ability to reason, all are expressions of God's image in you. Yes, you are fallen, but as God changes you, he repairs the broken image of himself in you.

The earth is full of God's glory. It reflects God's majesty, just as the moon reflects the glory of the sun when you can't see the sun directly. Of all the things in creation, nothing is better suited to display God's glory than you are—by loving, by building, by speaking the truth, in short, by being godly. You are a mirror reflecting God's majesty for all the earth to see. You're a cracked mirror, to be sure, but one day you'll be made whole, and all creation will rejoice.

> All living things look hopefully to you, and you give them food when they need it. You give them enough and satisfy the needs of all.
> Psalm 145:15–16 GNT

do something

The created world is a window through which you can glimpse the majesty of God. Have a look around. Listen. God speaks through his works. He reveals himself, just as surely as any artist reveals himself through his works of art.

words
to live by

Let every created thing give praise to the LORD, for he issued his command, and they came into being.
Psalm 148:5 NLT

The God who created, names and numbers the stars in the heavens also numbers the stars of my head. . . . He pays attention to very big things and to very small ones. What matters to me matters to Him, and that changes my life.
ELISABETH ELLIOT

Scientists have identified about one million species of insects. And they estimate that another eight million to thirty million species of insects are out there not yet identified. How's that for creativity?

In 1646, Bishop James Usher offered up an exact date that God began the work of Creation. Counting back from the genealogies in the Bible, Bishop Usher believed that the first day of Creation was October 22, 4004 B.C.

final thought

God, I cannot look at the world around me without praising the One who made it. You are more powerful than a waterfall. You are bigger than the heavens. And yet you care for me. Praise your holy name. Amen.

de·sire, noun

1. a longing or craving.
2. an expressed wish or request.
3. something desired.
4. **Biblical:** a passion for some object or goal; may be a passion for something good or a passion for something bad.
5. **Personal:** the yearnings and wants that determine what objectives a person pursues.

Bird Dogs and the Pursuit of Happiness

Delight yourself in the LORD; and He will
give you the desires of your heart.
Psalm 37:4 NASB

A trained quail dog has one desire that overshadows all others. Its deepest longing, its single passion is to go into the fields and forests and hunt quail. Nose to the ground, tail up, it scans the underbrush for the birds it was born and bred to find. Rabbits might scamper past, ground sparrows might flit around by the dozen, but nothing disturbs the bird dog's laserlike focus. It knows why it's here. And when it sees the white of a quail's head bobbing deep in the bushes, it locks onto it with a new focus and determination. As still as any statue, front paw lifted, tail arrow-straight, the dog waits for the command to flush the quarry: "Go get it!" This is what a bird dog lives for.

An average, untrained dog rambling through the woods is another thing altogether. Like the bird dog, it was born with a desire to hunt. But it isn't a focused desire. The dog chases every

words
to live by

squirrel into a tree, lunges at every bird that flutters up from the deep grass, barks at every lizard that presents itself. The woods offer the same stimuli to the quail dog. But the quail dog's desire is focused. A lesser quarry doesn't have the power to draw it off the trail.

You were born with a hunting instinct too. You're on a lifelong pursuit of happiness. That desire comes from God. It's not a bad thing. It calls you back to God, for the desire for happiness can be fulfilled only in a relationship with him. But the world offers one substitute desire after another: the desire for things, the desire for excitement, the desire for sex, the desire for control. You can make your own list; the point is, if you don't focus on what you're truly after, you might chase after every lesser desire and run right past the thing you're really hunting.

Ironically, when you tend to that truest desire—the desire for happiness in God—the lesser desires get fulfilled too. Materialism becomes gratitude for the things God has given you. The need for popularity becomes a healthy desire to be a genuine friend. The drive to succeed becomes the satisfaction of doing your best for the glory of God. Sexual desire is over-

> Christ is a most precious commodity, he is better than rubies or the most costly pearls; and we must part with our old gold, with our shining gold, our old sins, our most shining sins, or we must perish forever. Christ is to be sought and bought with any pains, at any price; we cannot buy this gold too dear. He is a jewel worth more than a thousand worlds, as all know who have him. Get him, and get all; miss him and miss all.
>
> **THOMAS BROOKS**

ruled by a desire for the intimacy of a godly marriage.

That's not to say that a person who has turned to God is forever free from misguided desires. Those lesser desires continue to present themselves as long as you're on earth. But it's a life-changing thing to realize that every desire is just a desire for happiness, and that the only genuine happiness grows out of a relationship with God. It serves as a filter on your experience. For a quail dog, the lure of the quail makes the lure of the ground sparrow irrelevant. Like that dog, you were born for one thing: happiness in God. So go get it.

> I am overwhelmed with joy in the LORD my God! For he has dressed me with the clothing of salvation and draped me in a robe of righteousness. I am like a bridegroom in his wedding suit or a bride with her jewels.
>
> Isaiah 61:10 NLT

do something

You are what you want. Don't let the world's substitute desires throw you off the trail of your truest desire. The only happiness that has any hope of lasting is the happiness that you find in knowing God. Every other desire will break its promise to you.

words
to live by

You have given him his heart's desire; you have answered his request.
Psalm 21:2 GNT

True saints have their minds, in the first place, inexpressibly pleased and delighted with the sweet ideas of the glorious and amiable nature of the things of God. And this is the spring of all their delights, and the cream of all their pleasures.
JONATHAN EDWARDS

In the New Testament the Greek word that is most frequently translated *desire* is used to mean both the righteous desire for the things of God and the sinful desire for the things of the flesh (sometimes translated "lust").

According to the Westminster Confession of Faith, the chief purpose of human beings is "to glorify God and enjoy him forever." John Piper has a slightly different version: The chief purpose of human beings, he says, is "to glorify God by enjoying him forever."

Final thought

God, I am too easily pleased. I let paltry little desires for earthly pleasures distract me from pursuing the everlasting pleasures that you offer for the taking. Amen.

dis·ci·ple, noun

1. one who embraces and assists in spreading the teachings of another.
2. an active adherent, as of a movement or philosophy.
3. a student or follower of a teacher.
4. *Biblical:* one of the twelve in Jesus' inner circle.
5. *Personal:* a person who has let go of the ordinary life in order to pursue the extraordinary life of imitating Christ.

The Upward Call

I run straight to the goal with purpose in every step. . . . I discipline my body like an athlete, training it to do what it should.

I Corinthians 9:26–27 NLT

The life of an Olympic athlete in training doesn't look very much like the lives of the rest of the world. Olympic athletes don't eat the same food. They don't sleep the same hours. If they're school age, their schooling is different. Hardly an hour of an Olympic athlete's day is the same as yours would be. In many regards, you could say that an Olympic athlete has left the world behind. But why? They are working for a goal that they value more than they value a "normal" life. They make sacrifices the rest of the world finds hard to understand. But an athlete competing at the highest levels might find it equally hard to understand why anyone else would settle for "normal."

To be a disciple of Jesus is to leave the world behind and go into training. A disciple is one who follows after a master—not casually, they way you might follow your favorite sports team, but

words
to live by

following strenuously, working hard to imitate or be like the master. Throughout the Gospels, Jesus gathered up his disciples with a simple command: "Follow me." And contained in that command to follow is a call to leave the world behind. It's a command to stop pursuing your own agenda and start following Christ, wherever he may lead.

Self-denial is an important part of discipleship. But self-denial isn't a good thing in itself; it's good only insofar as it frees up your energies, your time, even your emotions to follow after something better than self-interest. For an Olympic ice skater, getting up at four in the morning isn't the point; the point is getting up at four in the morning and training to win a gold medal. Discipleship is training too. You may not have to get up before daylight every day to be a disciple of Jesus, but you do have to be serious about training to be like him. And that training is going to cost something in earthly terms: It will cost you time, it will cost you some long-ingrained habits, it may cost you some friends. You know what the costs will be for you—or, if you don't, you'll soon find out if you decide to follow Christ.

> Do not scrutinize so closely whether you are doing much or little, ill or well, so long as what you do is not sinful and that you are heartily seeking to do everything for God. Try as far as you can to do everything well, but when it is done, do not think about it. Try, rather, to think of what is to be done next. Go on simply in the Lord's way, and do not torment yourself.
>
> SAINT FRANCIS DE SALES

You may have never thought of following Jesus as a skill. But discipleship does involve certain skills. You weren't born knowing how to pray or how to meditate on the truths of the Scriptures. You weren't born with a head full of Bible verses. Nor were you born with a heart to serve your fellow human beings. True, God changes your heart, and the Spirit teaches you to pray, but even so, Christ's command to follow him is a call to actively pursue him, to train hard to be like him, not just a call to passively receive God's benefits.

It's worth noting that the New Testament uses the word *Christian* three times, while it uses the word *disciple* 269 times. God's people, it seems, are identified not by the name they call themselves, but by their willingness to follow after their Master.

> Go, then, to all peoples everywhere and make them my disciples: baptize them in the name of the Father, the Son, and the Holy Spirit.
> **Matthew 28:19** GNT

do something

Jesus commands his disciples to deny themselves. That may seem harsh, but remember: He requires you to let go of the things of this world only so that you can take hold of something better. Is anything holding you back from following Jesus? Let it go. Leave it behind. In the pursuit of Christ, you'll get back more than you ever let go of.

words
to live by

The term *apostle* typically applies to a smaller subset of Christ's disciples—that inner circle consisting of the Twelve and a few others, the most notable of whom was the apostle Paul. The apostles are those individuals whom Jesus personally sent out to spread the Gospel to the world.

Dietrich Bonhoeffer distinguished between cheap grace—that is, grace without discipleship—and costly grace—grace that must be sought again and again. One of relatively few German ministers who stood up to the Nazis, Bonhoeffer was thrown in a Nazi prison, where he died.

Imitate me as I imitate Christ.
I Corinthians 11:1
GOD'S WORD

God does not want hearers and repeaters of words, but followers and doers, and this occurs in faith through love.
MARTIN LUTHER

final thought

God, I am ready to follow you. I don't want to watch from a safe distance. I want to be in the thick of things, going where you lead, growing more and more like you. Teach me and use me. I'm not going to turn back now. Amen.

The Upward Call

en·cour·age·ment, noun

1. an act of inspiring with courage, spirit, or confidence.
2. stimulating by assistance or approval.
3. an instance of emboldening, heartening, or reassuring.
4. *Biblical:* urging someone onward or helping them along.
5. *Personal:* persuading fellow believers to keep going when they feel like stopping.

Heartbreak Hill

Think of ways to encourage one another
to outbursts of love and good deeds.
Hebrews 10:24 NLT

Heartbreak Hill. It's the most famous section of the Boston Marathon. Here hardened athletes falter, daunted by this slope that seems to go on forever. Here grown men and women—world-class athletes—cry. Here the marathon is won and lost.

Heartbreak Hill isn't that steep, actually. But it's long. It stretches almost a mile on a gentle grade—up a little, up a little, up a little more. There's no dramatic moment, no sudden steepness that defeats everybody at once. It's the sheer length of it that saps the runner's will, one step at a time.

It couldn't come at a worse time. Even the best-trained athletes tend to "hit the wall" around mile twenty. The human body is very close to its limit at this point, and it takes an almost super-human act of the will to keep going, even under the best of

words
to live by

circumstances. On the Boston Marathon course, Heartbreak Hill starts just a few yards past mile marker twenty. Just when every muscle in the runner's body is screaming for relief. Just when the runner's mind is asking, "Why on earth are you doing this, anyway?" Just when the runner's will is at its lowest ebb, the road slopes. Up a little. Up a little. Up a little more.

> The best exercise for strengthening the heart is reaching down and lifting people up.
> **ERNEST BLEVINS**

If the runner is in top condition and has been having a good race, the first few steps may not seem so bad. But the hill just keeps on going. Every step is a little harder than the last, step after step after step. Heartbreak Hill gets to everyone eventually.

Even as the Hill destroys the runner's will, however, there's one thing that rebuilds the will to press on: the encouragement of the fans. Thousands and thousands of fans line both sides of the street for the entire length of Heartbreak Hill, shouting encouragement, holding up signs, offering cups of cool, refreshing water.

"You can do it." "The Hill will not defeat you!" "Run through the pain." "Keep going, it's worth it!"

While the runner's legs are saying that they can't go on, the fans remind them that they can. And every year, hundreds of Boston Marathoners say the same thing: They would have quit on Heartbreak Hill had it not been for the encouragement of the thousands of fans who cheered them on. For those runners, the fans on Heartbreak Hill literally saved the race for them.

That's how encouragement works. In the hard patches of life, when you're ready to quit, somebody comes alongside you and says, "Keep going, it's worth it," or "God has a great plan for you; don't give up now!" or just "I love you."

> Encourage one another day after day, as long as it is still called "Today," so that none of you will be hardened by the deceitfulness of sin.
> **Hebrews 3:13** NASB

Encouragement takes you out of that inner dialogue of defeat—"I can't do this . . . none of this matters anyway . . . I might as well drop out"—and brings you back to the reality of who you are in Christ. When discouragement saps your will and breaks your heart, a word of encouragement renews your will to keep pressing on.

do something

It's not all that hard to encourage another person. You don't have to offer any particular words of wisdom; you just have to pay attention. Whom do you know who's discouraged? Who is ready to give up on living the Christian life? Send them a note. Give them a call. Remind them that it's worth pressing on.

words
to live by

We encourage you, brothers and sisters, to instruct those who are not living right, cheer up those who are discouraged, help the weak, and be patient with everyone.

1 Thessalonians 5:14
GOD'S WORD

We can often better help another by fanning a glimmer of goodness than by censuring his faults.

EDMUND GIBSON

In the early Church, there was one disciple named Joseph who was so good at encouraging others that he was given a nickname, *Barnabas*, that is translated "Son of Encouragement." He is still remembered by that nickname almost two thousand years later.

Jesus was an encourager. "Take heart" (sometimes translated "be of good cheer") was a widely used phrase of encouragement. Jesus used this phrase on five different occasions, including once after his death and resurrection, when he appeared to the apostle Paul in prison.

final thought

God, give me eyes to see those who are discouraged. Give me a heart that desires to encourage them. Give me the words to lift them up and to spur them on to finish the race. Amen.

Heartbreak Hill

fel·low·ship, noun

1. friendly relationship; companionship.
2. community of interest or feeling.
3. an association of persons having similar tastes or interests.
4. communion, as between members of the same church.
5. **Biblical:** the bond of love between fellow Christians.
6. **Personal:** the sharing of a life with other believers.

As the Goose Flies

We who are strong ought to bear the weaknesses of those without strength and not just please ourselves. Each of us is to please his neighbor for his good, to his edification.
Romans 15:1–2 NASB

Lots of things can be the basis for a friendship—shared musical interests, players on the same sports team, next-door neighbors. But Christian fellowship is something different, something deeper. It's not just a common interest in church activities. Fellowship grows from a realization that Christians are many parts of a body with one Head: Jesus himself! The parts of the body need one another. They all work together toward the same goals. If one part of the body suffers, the other parts of the body suffer with it. If one part of the body is honored, the other parts of the body rejoice with it.

In the Bible, fellowship is all about sharing. In the book of Acts, the early Christians shared all things in common—their meals, their homes, their possessions. Christians today don't typically share all their possessions with one another in the same

words
to live by

way. But Christians are still called to share one anothers' burdens. As believers walk alongside one another, the long journey of life is easier for everybody. You are strengthened and energized when you share your friends' joys. You are encouraged and lifted up when friends share your sorrows.

Have you ever wondered why geese fly in a V formation? It's their way of bearing each others' burdens. Flying just behind its neighbor's outside wing, each goose faces less wind resistance and enjoys a smoother flight. At the same time, it leads the way for the goose that's next in line. Flying with the flock takes a lot less energy than flying alone.

> Love is the outpouring of one personality in fellowship with another personality.
> **OSWALD CHAMBERS**

But what about the lead goose, out on the point of the V? Who is easing the load for him? The lead goose is doing the most work, taking the full brunt of the wind resistance while everybody else has it easy, right? True, but here's the amazing thing: When the lead goose gets tired, it just peels off and goes to the back of the formation, where it can rest and get its strength back. A new goose takes a shift as flock leader.

As a Christian, you look forward to an eternity in which every burden will be lifted. Every tear will be wiped away. Your joy will be perfected, even as you will be perfected. In the meantime, God has given believers to one another. And as imperfect believers walk through this imperfect world, they can see each other through—and can make one anothers' joy full. When God commands you to fellowship with other Christians and to love one another, he is commanding you to be happy. It is through fellowship—with God and with other believers—that you find the happiness you seek in so many different ways. Strange that God would have to command Christians to do that which they most want to do.

Remember what God said about Adam before he had made Eve? "It is not good for man to be alone." You were made for fellowship. You find completeness in loving and fellowshiping with others.

> Be devoted to each other like a loving family. Excel in showing respect for each other.
>
> **Romans 12:10** GOD'S WORD

do something

Fellowship doesn't just happen. You have to be intentional about it. Plan a regular time of fellowship time with Christian friends two or three times a month. Share a meal together. Share your concerns and your hopes with one another. Enjoy one another. That's the key, really. As you enjoy spending time with your Christian friends, your relationships will deepen, and God will knit your hearts together.

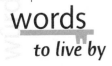

words
to live by

As iron sharpens iron, a friend sharpens a friend.
Proverbs 27:17 NLT

True friends don't spend time gazing into each other's eyes. They may show great tenderness towards each other, but they face in the same direction—towards common projects, goals—above all, towards a common Lord.
C. S. LEWIS

Harvard researchers have found that, for senior citizens, friendship and social activities result in longer life. According to this study, friendship contributes to longevity just as much as regular exercise does.

Eating together has always been an important part of fellowship and friendship. In fact, the word *companion* comes from a Latin word meaning "one to eat bread with."

final thought

The relationship between Christians is like the relationship between Christians is like the relationship between the leaves on a vine. In order to be healthy, each leaf needs the other leaves. But most of all, each leaf needs the vine.

for·give, verb

1. to grant free pardon for or remission of an offense or debt.
2. to give up all claim on account of a debt or obligation.
3. to cease to feel resentment against.
4. **Biblical:** to voluntarily release a person over which one has legal or actual control.
5. **Personal:** to let go of the wrongs another person has done against you.

Forgive us the wrongs we have done, as we forgive the wrongs that others have done to us.
Matthew 6:12 GNT

Imagine you let a friend borrow your car. He totals it. He's got no money to pay for the damage, no way to repay the debt he owes you. So you forgive the debt. But at school the next week, you see that same friend jabbing a finger in the face of another student, shouting, "Give me my money now! When I loan a person lunch money, I expect to be paid back." What would you think of such a person?

Jesus once told a similar parable about forgiveness: A king was settling up old accounts, collecting money he had loaned to his slaves in the past. One of his slaves owed him ten thousand talents. That would be millions of dollars in today's money. The servant could never pay such an enormous debt. So the king ordered that the man be sold into slavery along with his wife and all his children so that part of his debt should be paid.

words
to live by

The slave was frantic. He fell to his knees and begged for mercy. He pleaded for another chance, promising to repay the money somehow. The king took pity on him at last. Not only did he give the slave another chance, but he forgave the entire debt. He wiped the slave's account clean.

So far so good. The slave was out of jail, his account was balanced, things were looking up again. But then the slave had a very bad idea. This man who had just been forgiven millions of dollars went and found a fellow slave who owed him a hundred denarii. That would be no more than a few dol-

> Forgiveness does not mean ignoring what has been done or putting a false label on an evil act. It means, rather, that the evil act no longer remains as a barrier to the relationship.
> MARTIN LUTHER KING JR.

lars, a tiny fraction of his own forgiven debt. "Pay up!" he demanded, and he began to choke the other slave. The debtor fell to the ground and begged for mercy. But the first slave refused to show any. He had the man thrown into jail. That was his right under the law, after all.

When the other slaves told the king what had happened, he was enraged. He called the first slave before him again and sent him to prison until he could repay his debt.

Jesus ended this parable with a chilling statement: "So shall my heavenly father also do to you if each of you does not forgive his brother from your heart." Christians have been for-given a huge sin debt. God has released them and sent their sins away. It doesn't make sense, then, for Christians to hold on

oness grace mercy love faith goodness truth freedom hope
rgiveness peace humble holiness obey repent perfect submit
rve fellowship comforter transformed noble character church

to other people's sin, to try to keep the people in the same bondage they themselves have been released from.

Every wrong another person commits against you is like a little debt. It's as if that person owes you something. That's why some translations of the Lord's Prayer say "forgive us our debts as we forgive our debtors." The problem is, it's a debt you can never collect on. The only real way the account can be settled is for you to forgive. That's not always easy. But it's easier than carrying around a load of resentment and bitterness. If you have had your own slate wiped clean, you have the power to let go of another person's sin—and the power to release the sinner.

> Be kind to one another, tenderhearted, forgiving one another, even as God in Christ forgave you.
> **Ephesians 4:32 NKJV**

do something

Your motive for forgiving other people is the knowledge that you've been forgiven yourself. And besides, carrying around somebody else's sin doesn't do you any good. It's like chewing on somebody else's dirty sock: What's the point?

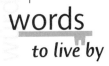

words
to live by

Oh, what joy for those whose rebellion is forgiven, whose sin is put out of sight!
Psalm 32:1 NLT

He that cannot forgive others, breaks the bridge over which he himself must pass if he would ever reach heaven; for everyone has need to be forgiven.
LORD HERBERT

⌐ One biblical word for *forgive* is literally translated "to send away." In the Israelites' scapegoat ritual, the high priest put both hands on the head of a goat and confessed the sins of the people. The goat was then driven into the wilderness, carrying the people's sins with it.

⌐ Medical studies show that people who exercise a forgiving spirit are healthier than those who choose to hold on to bitterness and old hurts. These studies show that forgivers aren't just mentally and emotionally healthier, but physically healthier as well.

 final thought

God, you have forgiven me so much. Forgive me again for refusing to forgive those who have wronged me. I have no right to hold on to the sins of others when you have sent my own sins so far away. Amen.

Letting Go

93

gen·er·os·i·ty, noun

1. a readiness or liberality in giving.
2. the freedom from meanness or smallness of mind or character.
3. an act of unselfishness.
4. **Biblical:** a giving spirit that results from a single-minded commitment to the work of God.
5. **Personal:** an open-heartedness that results from an awareness of your own blessedness.

Paying Forward

Give, and you will receive. A large quantity, pressed together, shaken down, and running over will be put into your pocket. The standards you use for others will be applied to you.
Luke 6:38 GOD'S WORD

In 1995, the University of Southern Mississippi received a very surprising gift: $150,000 from a washerwoman named Oseola McCarty. Everyone who knew Ms. McCarty thought she was poor. After all, she was eighty-seven years old and still working her fingers to the bone, washing and ironing other people's clothes just as she had for the last seventy-five years. She had never owned a car; she walked everywhere she went. Only recently had she gotten an air conditioner to take the edge off the Mississippi summers, but even then, she only ran it when she had company over.

That was Ms. McCarty's way. She always thought of her own possessions in terms of how she might use them to bless others. She never spent money on herself—just the bare minimum. Instead, she put away every cent she could, saving a few dollars

words
to live by

here, a few dollars there for seventy-five years. Then, at the age of eighty-seven, she gave her life savings away—some to her church, some to her relatives, and the $150,000 gift to the university.

Of all the gifts that Ms. McCarty gave, the gift to the university was the one that truly changed her life. Though she had left her native South only once in her first eighty-seven years, in the year after she made her gift to the university, she made seven trips to New York City, seven trips to Washington, D.C., and many other trips to faraway places to receive awards and do media interviews. Every major network did a story on Ms. McCarty and her amazing gift. People all over the world were astonished at the kindness and generosity of this humble woman.

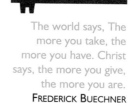

The world says, The more you take, the more you have. Christ says, the more you give, the more you are.
FREDERICK BUECHNER

The readers of the largest newspaper in the state of Mississippi named Ms. McCarty Mississippi's Humanitarian of the Century. Not only Southern Mississippi, but also Harvard University granted honorary doctorates to Ms. McCarty in honor of her commitment to education. Ms. McCarty, by the way, never made it past sixth grade. It wasn't that she did poorly in school or didn't value education. She gave up her chance at an education because she had a sick aunt who needed care. Even as a young girl, she was in the habit of giving.

Oseola McCarty died in 1999. But her legacy lives on. Her money, saved a few dollars at a time over a long and fruitful life, now funds a scholarship that helps deserving African-American students go to college. Ms. McCarty said, "I just want the scholarship to go to some child who needs it, to whoever is not able to help their children. I'm too old to get an education, but they can."

Jesus assured his followers that the more they give, the more they receive. It's one of the paradoxes of the Christian life: You give more, you have more. It's like having your cake and eating it too. As you learn to keep a loose grip on your possessions, even your time, you're better able to get a grip on the things that matter more.

> Some give freely, yet grow all the richer; others withhold what is due, and only suffer want.
>
> Proverbs 11:24 NRSV

do something

Generosity grows out of gratitude. As you realize how much you've been given, you become more and more glad to give to others. The Bible promises that when you give, you receive back even more. There's another reason to be generous. Give a little. See if you aren't blessed as a result of your generosity.

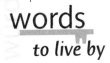

words
to live by

In 1783, a bad harvest limited food supplies. However, General Lafayette, hero of the American Revolution, had plenty of grain. A friend remarked that increased grain prices made it a good time to sell. But Lafayette, thinking of the hungry peasants, answered, "No, now is a good time to give."

Some of the most famous givers in the New Testament were the members of the Macedonian church. In spite of affliction and deep poverty, their joy overflowed—and so did their generosity. Paul's testimony to their giving spirit (2 Corinthians 8:1–5) keeps their memory alive even today.

Instruct them to do good, to be rich in good works, to be generous and ready to share, storing up for themselves the treasure of a good foundation for the future, so that they may take hold of that which is life indeed.

1 Timothy 6:18–19
NASB

The measure of a life, after all, is not its duration, but its donation.
CORRIE TEN BOOM

final thought

God, you have blessed me richly in many ways. Help me to love other people more than I love my possessions or my own time. May I give of myself, in thanks to the One who gave himself for me. Amen.

God's will, noun

1. the omnipotent wish or desire of God.
2. the assertion of God's choice.
3. God's wish carried out.
4. **Biblical:** God's desire or plan for all of his creation.
5. **Personal:** God's big picture, into which your life fits, from tiny details to world-wide movements.

Right Driving

We know that in all things God works for the good of those who love him, who have been called according to his purpose.

Romans 8:28 NIV

You're making a nighttime road trip. Your headlights illuminate the road as far as the next curve. A map light is just bright enough for you to track your progress on a state map. Would you say you can see where you're going? Well, yes and no. You can't actually see your destination. Nor can you see every bend, every obstacle that lies between you and the end of your trip. But you can see enough to keep moving toward your destination. And the map gives you the big picture, enough to see that you're on the right road.

Seeking God's will for your life is a little bit like that nighttime road trip. What is God's will for your life ten years from now? Where will you be? What will you be doing? There's no way of knowing. You can only live by the light God gives today.

words
to live by

"God's will" is a pretty big concept to try to wrap your brain around. It helps to break it into its three parts. The first part is sometimes called God's "providential will." This is the big, big picture: everything God is accomplishing through all of human history, and even beyond. He redeems his people. He defeats Satan. He conquers sin and death. This big picture is mapped by the Bible. No scheme of Satan, no human mistake, not even the most heinous sin can throw God's providential will off track.

"For My thoughts are not your thoughts, nor are your ways My ways," says the LORD.
Isaiah 55:8 NKJV

The second aspect of God's will is his "moral will." These are the "shalts" and the "shalt nots." It is God's will that you not cheat or lie or steal. It is God's will that you show kindness to others, that you honor your parents. If God's providential will is the big-picture roadmap, you might think of God's moral will as your headlights, keeping you on the path in the here and now. God's will can seem mysterious, but when it comes to his moral will, it's almost never a mystery. You know the difference between right and wrong. Life comes at you one decision at a time, and the vast majority of those decisions are small: *Do I tell a little lie? Do I stand up for what's right?* String together a few bad decisions, and you might find yourself in the ditch.

Finally, there's God's "personal will" for your life. Where does he want you to go to college? Whom does he want you to marry? What career does he have for you? This is the good stuff, isn't it? This is what you really mean when you talk about seeking God's will for your life. But this is probably the most mysterious aspect of God's will. Only God knows what's beyond the next curve. In another way, however, it's not as mysterious as it seems. When the time comes for the big decisions, God provides the light you need, and often in very mundane ways—through your circumstances, your abilities, your desires, the advice of those who are older and wiser.

> Show me the path where I should walk, O LORD; point out the right road for me to follow.
> Psalm 25:4 NLT

You can only act on what you can see. But you can see enough. You can see up to the next curve. Stay on the road. And when those big moments of decision come along, they'll be lit too.

do something

Trying to see God's will for your future can be intimidating. But here's good news: God's will for right this minute isn't so hard to figure out. He wants you to love him with all your heart, soul, mind, and strength, and he wants you to love your neighbor as yourself. That ought to keep you busy; the future you can leave to God.

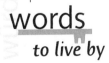

words
to live by

When the Bible speaks of *God's will*, one of the most common images is that of a "way" or a "path." In the familiar verse "My ways are not your ways," the word *ways* means "paths" or "roads." To seek God's will is to seek road signs on the path.

In important times of decision, God revealed his will to the Israelites through special stones called the Urim and Thummim. It is not known exactly how the priests used them; perhaps they cast them like dice. When they weren't being used, they decorated the breastplate of the High Priest.

The human mind plans the way, but the Lord directs the steps.
Proverbs 16:9 NRSV

When God is involved, anything can happen. . . . Be open. Stay that way. God has a beautiful way of bringing good vibrations out of broken chords.
CHARLES SWINDOLL

Final thought

God, I know your will is perfect. Give me the light I need to stay on the path you have laid out for me. Your will be done. Amen.

Night Driving

God's Word, noun

1. a manifestation of the mind and will of God.
2. the authoritative utterance of God.
3. the Bible, the sacred writings of the Christian religion.
4. *Biblical:* the specific communications of God to human beings.
5. *Personal:* the truths of the Bible that have the power to transform.

Yesterday, Today, and Tomorrow

Your word is a lamp for my feet
and a light for my path.
Psalm 119:105 NLT

The celebrity magazines in the grocery checkout lane can be pretty hard to resist. Who's got a new movie coming out? What were the stars wearing at the Grammy Awards? Who's dating whom? It's fun to feel like you're "in the know" about the lives of your favorite celebrities. But when you read the same magazine six months later in your dentist's waiting room, it's a very different experience, isn't it? The "Sizzling Summer Blockbusters" are now just more DVDs lining the walls of the video store. "Hollywood's Hottest New Couple" has broken up and paired off again with new partners since that issue came out. *Yawn.* You dig back into the magazine pile for something more interesting.

God's Word is different. "The grass withers, the flower fades, but the word of our God stands forever" (Isaiah 40:8 NASB). Time gobbles up everything the world has to offer. Yesterday's news is

words
to live by

dead and gone. Make room for the next big thing. But the Word of God is solid, real, and no less relevant today than it was two thousand years ago. It stands outside of time.

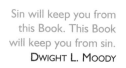

Sin will keep you from this Book. This Book will keep you from sin.
DWIGHT L. MOODY

As a teen, you live with constant pressure to be up to the minute in every aspect of your life—to wear the latest styles, to talk the latest slang from the latest big TV show, to know the latest gossip from school. It's as if your real self is being buried under all these external things that change so quickly you can hardly keep up.

The Word of God takes you outside of all that. It says, "Look here: Here's who you really are. Forget about your clothes for a minute. Forget about school gossip. Forget about the fight you just had with your parents. If you'll slow down for a little while, you can see who you really are, down at the bedrock of your self—and what God plans to do about it. You can come back later to how you dress, how you talk, how you spend your time. But start here."

While the world does its best to conform you to itself, God's Word transforms you. It plants you deep in the solid ground of truth; instead of floating on every new trend or new idea that blows through, you stand firm. You have a perspective from which to make sense of the things the world sends your way. Does that mean you'll reject every new fashion and start speaking like King James? Of course not. But it does mean that you'll feel a new freedom to ignore those styles of dress or speech that don't suit you or don't honor God.

There's something very satisfying in the solidity that comes from being rooted in the Word of God. The world offers very little certainty. How many times have you done a Web search only to find that the page you were looking for was no longer available? Not so with God's Word. It's the same yesterday, today, and forever.

> In the beginning was the Word, and the Word was with God, and the Word was God.
>
> John 1:1 NASB

do something

You're at a time of life when you're trying to "find" yourself. There's no better place to start looking than in the Word of God. Here you will see who you are before your Creator. And, by the way, it's very good news. How much time do you spend reading and meditating on God's Word? Chew on it. Watch yourself grow more solid. You might surprise yourself.

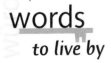

words
to live by

All Scripture is inspired by God and is useful to teach us what is true and to make us realize what is wrong in our lives. It straightens us out and teaches us to do what is right.
2 Timothy 3:16 NLT

Of all commentaries upon the Scriptures, good examples are the best and the liveliest.
JOHN DONNE

Did you know that the Bible was once a banned book in Christian countries? In the Middle Ages, church leaders were reluctant to allow church members to read the Bible without the guidance of priests. So the Bible was added to the Church's list of forbidden books.

Deuteronomy 6:8 commands God's people "tie [God's words] as symbols on your hands and bind them on your foreheads" (NIV). This gave rise to *phylacteries*, little leather pouches containing pieces of paper on which Scriptures are written. Many Jews still wear phylacteries tied around their heads or around their arms.

Final thought

God, the world puts so many things in front of me that distract me from your word. Help me to see through the glitter and clutter and to focus on what really matters. Amen.

dness grace mercy love faith goodness truth freedom joy
orgiveness peace humble holiness obey repent perfect submit
erve fellowship comforter transformed noble character church

grace · grace · grace · grace · grace · grace

grace, noun

1. elegance of beauty, form, motion, or manner.
2. a manifestation of favor, especially by a superior.
3. mercy, clemency, or pardon.
4. *Biblical:* the saving kindness of God.
5. *Personal:* God's willingness to embrace even those who push him away.

By grace you have been saved through faith, and this is not your own doing; it is the gift of God—not the result of works, so that no one may boast.
Ephesians 2:8–9 NRSV

He had demanded his inheritance early. A son could hardly throw a more painful insult in a father's face. It was as if he had said, "Hey, old man, if you aren't planning to die soon, just let me have my cash so I can get on with my life without you." Father could have disowned him. Most fathers would have. Not this father. He gave his son the inheritance he asked for, then sent him on his way with a blessing.

Life was good in the big city. He was the life of the party. His pockets bulged with money. He treated everyone to the finest food and drink. He had more friends than he could shake a stick at. But the money didn't last. And as soon as the money was gone, the friends were gone too.

words
to live by

He got a job feeding pigs at a nearby farm, but it paid almost nothing. He ended up staying with the pigs in their shelter. The pigs' slop bucket usually contained some decent scraps from the farmer's table, so he was able to get by.

It doesn't take many days of living with pigs and eating pig slop before a person starts to feel homesick. It could be that one morning, while chewing on a piece of soggy toast he had wrestled from an especially nasty sow, he started thinking about the life he had left behind. *Even Father's servants live better than this*, he thought—*a hundred times better. They get three meals a day, a warm place to sleep, a kindly master to serve.* He realized what he should do. He couldn't go back and ask to be restored to his place in the family. But perhaps his father would hire him as a servant.

> There is nothing but God's grace. We walk upon it; we breathe it; we live and die by it; it makes the nails and axles of the universe; and a puppy in pajamas prefers self-conceit.
> ROBERT LOUIS STEVENSON

He left that very morning. It was a half-day's walk back home, and the whole way he might have practiced his speech: "Father, I have sinned against you. I am no longer worthy to be called your son. But if you'll let me join the ranks of your servants, I'll be the best servant you have ever had."

His father was watching the road from his high window, just as he had every day since his son had left home. In the distance he saw a traveler with the same loping stride as his lost son. The traveler's head was bowed—that wasn't like his son—

and the tattered clothes didn't look like something his style-conscious son would wear. But still . . . there was something about that traveler.

The father tore down the steps and burst through the front door at a dead run toward the ragged traveler. The servants, worried that their master had lost his mind, took off after him. By the time they caught up, he had the traveler in a bear hug, and they heard him speak in a hoarse, tear-choked whisper, "Servant? Never! You're my son." He turned to his servants and shouted, "Look at my son! He was dead, but now he's alive! Put rings on his fingers. Dress him in the finest clothes. Tonight we're having a feast to celebrate his return!"

> Surely He scorns the scornful, but gives grace to the humble.
> **Proverbs 3:34** NKJV

That's grace: No matter what you've done, no matter what you've become, no matter how you've rebelled against God, he stoops down and says, "None of that matters. You are my child, and I love you."

do something

Do you ever run away from God? Do you ever push him away? The good news of the gospel is that when you're tired of running, when you realize you need God after all, he's there with open arms. He is the God of grace. It makes no difference how deep a hole you've dug for yourself; when he reaches down to raise you up, his arm is always long enough.

words
to live by

Now I commit you to God, and to the word of his grace, which can build you up and give you an inheritance among all those who are sanctified.
Acts 20:32 NIV

Reality, in fact, is always something you couldn't have guessed. That's one of the reasons I believe Christianity. It's a religion you couldn't have guessed.
C. S. Lewis

⊤ Grace is really just one of many manifestations of love. This is Donald Barnhouse's helpful definition of grace as it relates to other kinds of love: "Love that goes upward is worship; love that goes outward is affection; love that stoops is grace."

⊤ The main New Testament word for grace is *charis*, which means "gift." The word is also related to beauty or attractiveness. The word *charis* also gives rise to the English word *charisma*. A charismatic person is gifted and attracts others.

final thought

God, even though you let me run, you always chase me down. God, you know how rebellious I can be. My sin is great; your grace is greater. I praise your name. Amen.

heav·en, noun

1. the abode of God, the angels, and the souls of the righteous after death.
2. a state or place of extreme happiness.
3. the sky, firmament, or expanse of space surrounding the earth; often, heavens.
4. *Biblical:* the dwelling place of God.
5. *Personal:* the Christian's true home.

Weighty Topic

They will never be hungry or thirsty again. Neither the sun nor any burning heat will ever overcome them. . . . God will wipe every tear from their eyes.

Revelation 7:16–17 GOD'S WORD

Think about the pictures you see of heaven. Everything seems light, fluffy, insubstantial. Usually there are people in white robes bouncing from cloud to cloud, strumming on harps. The truth is, if heaven is very much like the pictures you see, it doesn't seem like it would be all that much fun. Sure, walking on clouds would be very cool at first, but for all eternity? Eternity is so far beyond the human imagination that any attempt to picture it falls short. And so pictures of heaven, even when they're just mental pictures, tend to make heaven seem unreal and insubstantial.

The key to heaven is the presence of God. Heaven is the place where all barriers between you and God are gone. You will enjoy God completely, even as God enjoys you. But that's hard to imagine too. Maybe the best you can do is to imagine a place

words
to live by

that's free from everything that makes it hard to be a human being. There will be no more sadness, no more frustration, no more temptation, no more disappointment.

As long as you're on earth, there's always a gap between you and the happiness and fulfillment you seek. As a teen, you're very aware of that gap. You've left childhood behind, but the independence of adulthood is still out of reach. You can see it, but you aren't there yet. Some "key to happiness" is always just around the corner. You long for a driver's license, convinced that all your troubles will be over when you don't have to depend on anybody else to drive you around. Then you get your license, and it's not all it's cracked up to be. So you decide that graduating from high school is the real key to happiness. But that doesn't quite do it either, so you set your sights on college.

> The tragedies that now blacken and darken the very air of heaven for us, will sink into their places in a scheme so august, so magnificent, so joyful, that we shall laugh for wonder and delight.
> ARTHUR C. BACON

If you set your sights on the things of the world, happiness and fulfillment will always be just out of reach. Heaven is the answer to all that. The gap is closed at last: presence with God means there's nothing standing between you and happiness.

You're a teen. You have a whole life ahead of you. Why think about the afterlife? In fact, heaven is what puts this life in perspective. Even if you've got a hundred years ahead of you, in the big picture it's only a blink. That realization can change your life.

grace mercy love faith goodness truth freedom hope
forgiveness peace humble holiness obey repent perfect submit
serve fellowship comforter transformed noble character church

heaven · heav·en · heav·en · heav·en · heav·en · heav·en

Paul, writing about life's challenges, put it this way: "Momentary, light affliction is producing for us an eternal weight of glory far beyond all comparison" (2 Corinthians 4:17 NASB). You probably aren't enduring the same kind of suffering that Paul did. But you do experience temptation—the false promise that you can be happy now if you'll just trade long-term happiness for short-term pleasure. You experience frustration, sadness, disappointment, the feeling that you just aren't good enough. It's real. It hurts. There's no question about that. Paul doesn't say his sufferings are imaginary. He says they're light and momentary when compared to the eternal weight of glory. Think about a feather. A feather is real, but compared to a boulder it seems pretty insubstantial. The hardships and temptations of life are feathers. But eternal life—eternal life is a boulder.

> You have been raised to life with Christ, so set your hearts on the things that are in heaven, where Christ sits on his throne at the right side of God.
> **Colossians 3:1** GNT

do something

When you're living on earth, the things of earth seem more real, more substantial than the things of heaven. The ground below your feet—what could seem more real and solid than that? But compared to heaven, the world around you is as light as a feather. Remember what Paul said: The frustrations and difficulties of life on earth are nothing compared to the glory that awaits in heaven.

words
to live by

Rejoice and be glad, for
your reward in heaven
is great.
Matthew 5:12 NASB

The Christians who did
most for the present
world were precisely
those who thought
most of the next. It is
since Christians have
begun thinking less of
the other world that
they have become so
ineffective in this. Aim
at heaven and you get
earth thrown in; aim at
earth and you get
neither.
C. S. LEWIS

Most religions have some
notion of heaven. In Buddhism,
heaven is the absence of desire. In
Hinduism and Islam, heaven is the
place where all fleshly desires are
satisfied. In the heaven of the
Bible, the most important fact is
God's presence, the true fulfillment of your desires.

The Bible describes the gates of
heaven as being carved from pearl.
And elsewhere, Jesus told Peter he
would give him the keys to heaven
and hell. Somebody put the two
together, and we got Saint Peter
keeping the keys of the Pearly
Gates.

final thought

God, because I can't see heaven, sometimes I forget that this world
isn't all there is. Help me to remember that this earth is not my
home. Help me to feel the eternal weight of glory. Amen.

A Weighty Topic

ho·li·ness, noun

1. a state of being specially recognized as or declared sacred by religious use or authority.
2. dedication or devotion to the service of God, the church, or religion.
3. saintliness; godliness; piety; devotion.
4. **Biblical:** the state of being separated unto God, displaying the personal conduct befitting one who is so separated.
5. **Personal:** wholeness, being restored to your original purpose as an image-bearer of God.

Don't copy the behavior and customs of
this world, but let God transform you
into a new person by changing the way
you think. Then you will know
what God wants you to do.
Romans 12:2 NLT

Imagine living in a world where everyone walks with a limp. The mailman limps. Your parents limp. The principal of your school limps. Even the stars of major motion pictures limp. Now imagine that your leg is healed, and you no longer have to limp. Suddenly you can walk straight, and you realize that human beings weren't meant to walk with a limp. Even your back feels better. It's the first time it's ever occurred to you that a lifetime of limping had given you a permanent backache. You thought that was just how you were supposed to feel.

But as you return to your day-to-day life, you find yourself slipping back into your old way of walking. You've been limping for as long as you could walk, after all. It's not that you *can't* walk straight. When you're paying attention, making a conscious effort, you can walk straight, and it feels great. Before, you

words
to live by

couldn't do that no matter how hard you tried. But face it—much of your life is lived on auto-pilot, and old habits die hard.

Besides, you get more than your share of funny looks when you walk around without a limp. The people either think you're crazy or they think you're just showing off, especially the friends who knew you when you walked just like them. To some you try to explain why you walk this way, but it's discouraging when people look at you like you have two heads. Sometimes you feel like giving up. You quit trying and limp around for days at a time. Then you can feel that old backache creeping back in.

> We have learned to live with unholiness and have come to look upon it as the natural and expected thing.
> **A. W. Tozer**

You find a few other straight-walkers, and that's a help. You remind each other that you were never meant to walk with a limp. You help one another to walk straight, and you celebrate the joys of a life that's free from that nagging backache. Eventually, your new habits begin to displace the old. But as long as you live in the world of the limpers, it's a constant struggle.

Holiness is a little bit like being a straight-walker in a world full of limpers. Holiness is wholeness. To be made holy is to be made well. In a fallen, broken world, wholeness looks strange, just as a normal, healthy stride would look strange in a world where everybody limps. Holiness is being set apart from the world in order to be made whole. Or, to put it another way, it's being set apart from the world because you've been made whole.

That separateness is demonstrated by a desire to obey God, to live differently from the world, with its devotion to self and pleasure. Holiness isn't just a matter of figuring out the rules and sticking to them. Holiness is reflecting the image of God in a world where that image has been shattered. God says, "Be holy, because I, the Lord your God, am holy" (Leviticus 19:2 GNT). That's what you're here for: to look like God.

> Blessed are the pure in heart, for they will see God.
> Matthew 5:8 NIV

do something

Holiness begins with the healing touch of God. But in practical terms, it takes practice. Some of the time, you'll limp around like everybody else. But as you stick with it, as you live out a commitment to holiness, it will get easier—not just because it becomes a habit, but because there's solid joy in fulfilling the purpose you were created for.

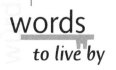

words
to live by

Those who say they live in God should live their lives as Christ did.
I John 2:6 NLT

A holy life is not an ascetic, or gloomy, or solitary life, but a life regulated by divine truth and faithful in Christian duty. It is living above the world while we are still in it.
TRYON EDWARDS

The word *holy* in the New Testament means "set apart." The word translated *saint* comes from the same word; it means "holy one" or "one who is set apart." The apostle Paul referred to all Christians as saints. All Christians are called to be set apart and holy.

Sometimes a desire for holiness drifts into legalism, the submission to rules made by human beings rather than God. Legalism has produced some strange rules. Some second-century Christians, for instance, thought anyone who was serious about holiness shouldn't sleep on a pillow, eat white bread, or shave.

final thought

God, you have set me apart to live differently from the rest of the world. Forgive me when I let myself be conformed to the world's ways. Strengthen my will to be holy like you. Amen.

A Life Apart

uness grace mercy love faith goodness truth freedom hope
orgiveness peace humble holiness obey repent perfect submit
erve fellowship comforter transformed noble character church

Holy Spirit, noun

1. the spirit of God.
2. the third person of the Trinity.
3. **Biblical:** the power of God in action.
4. **Personal:** the person of God that empowers the believer to live a God-pleasing life.

The Ghost in the Machine

I will ask the Father, and he will give you another Advocate, to be with you forever. This is the Spirit of truth.
John 14:16–17 NRSV

Have you ever seen the insides of a computer? The intricacies and complexities of the silver circuitry twisting and snaking across the shiny green of the motherboard, the spiny black rows of RAM, the shiny disks, the sparse black square of the processor—just looking at it you can sense the incredible potential for storing, managing, and calculating vast amounts of data.

But for all its potential, a computer is just an expensive doorstop if it has no power source. A computer can't power itself. In the same way, the truths of Christianity can't power themselves apart from the work of the Holy Spirit. Study the Bible as much as you like. Memorize all the shalts and shalt-nots and do your best to live by them. But without the power of the Holy Spirit, your faith is as dead as a computer with no battery or power cord.

words
to live by

The Holy Spirit is God—not a mist, not a feeling, not an idea. God is the Father, the Son, and the Holy Spirit. And it is as the Holy Spirit that God works through the lives of his people.

Take the apostles, for example. They experienced something you'll never experience: They saw Jesus— God the Son—in the flesh. They heard him preach and teach. They saw him perform miracles. He washed their feet. If anybody were in a position to live out the power of faith in Christ, it should be these guys, right? Well, not exactly. Most of the time they seemed a little confused by the things Jesus was telling them. They weren't especially humble. They weren't especially wise. They weren't especially brave. After Jesus died on the cross, the apostles began to melt back into their society. It seemed they would finish with more of a whimper than a bang.

We must not be content to be cleansed from sin; we must be filled with the Spirit.

JOHN FLETCHER

But then something remarkable happened. The risen Christ appeared to those same apostles and promised to baptize them with the Holy Spirit: "but you will receive power when the Holy Spirit has come to you." When the Holy Spirit came, it was as if all the circuitry that Jesus had laid down during his earthly ministry suddenly had power coursing through it. It was finally plugged in. The apostles, who had fled in fear when Jesus faced death, now proclaimed Christ boldly all over the known world, heedless of the consequences. The apostles who just didn't get it when Christ told them of the kingdom of God now brought people into the kingdom of God by the thousands. And the world was never the same.

The Holy Spirit is God's power in action. It was the Spirit who set creation in motion: "The Spirit of God was moving over the surface of the waters" (Genesis 1:2 NASB). It was the Spirit who spoke the Scriptures. It was the Spirit that added three thousand people to the Church at Pentecost. It's an awesome thing to think about: The same Spirit lives in every Christian. It would have been a great blessing to know God the Son when he lived on earth as a man. But it's just as great a blessing to know God the Spirit.

> Don't you know that you are God's temple and that God's Spirit lives in you?
> I Corinthians 3:16
> GOD'S WORD

do something

Apart from the Spirit, you don't have it in you to live the Christian life. You can't make any real sense out of the Bible. You can't bring anybody to Christ. But when the Holy Spirit begins to work in you and through you, suddenly your efforts to learn, to serve, to witness, to live a godly life all have meaning.

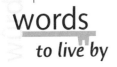

words
to live by

May the God of hope fill you with all joy and peace in believing, that you may abound in hope by the power of the Holy Spirit.
Romans 15:13 NKJV

Every time we say, "I believe in the Holy Spirit," we mean that we believe that there is a living God able and willing to enter human personality and change it.
J. B. PHILLIPS

In his book *The Names of the Holy Spirit*, Ray Pritchard lists eighty-seven names the Bible uses to refer to the Holy Spirit. Among them are the Comforter, the Seal, the Spirit of Fire, the Spirit of Grace, the Spirit of Holiness, and the Oil of Joy.

The most well-known outpouring of the Holy Spirit was at Pentecost. By the Spirit's power, the disciples preached, and the foreigners in the crowd heard the words in their own language. It was the first instance of 'speaking in tongues'—but some onlookers mistook the disciples' strange speech for drunkenness.

final thought

God, apart from your power, all religion is empty ritual. Apart from your wisdom, even the Scriptures are just words on a page. Apart from your Comfort, all comfort is meaningless. Make your power known in my life. Amen.

hope, noun

1. the feeling that what is desired is also possible, or that events might turn out for the best.
2. a particular instance of this feeling.
3. grounds for this feeling in a particular instance.
4. **Biblical:** a favorable expectation, based on the faithfulness of God.
5. **Personal:** a forward-looking confidence in God's perfect plan.

The Orthodontic Gospel

You are my hope, O Lord GOD; you
are my trust from my youth.
Psalm 71:5 NKJV

If you have ever had braces, you know a thing or two about hope. The experience of having your teeth straightened ranges from mildly annoying to downright painful. Sometimes it feels as if a daylong match of tug-of-war is going on inside your mouth. Those metal edges can be rough on the tender inside of your cheek. Also, you look kind of funny with a mouth full of metal. And don't forget the food that's always getting stuck between the wires at the most inconvenient moments—right before your class presentation, for instance.

Why would you put up with that kind of aggravation? You put up with it because you know that if you can just live with the little annoyances and play through the pain for a while, you'll be rewarded with a million-dollar smile that should last the rest of your life. Without that hope of reward, you'd never let anybody

words
to live by

invade your mouth with metal and rubber bands and cement and plastic for a year or more. That's hope in action: the ability to press through today's hardships because you know they are part of a larger plan—a plan that will result in rewards that far outweigh the hardships.

Hope is a word you hear all the time. "I hope I win the lottery." "I hope the teacher doesn't call on me today." "I hope our team wins the championship this year." In everyday use, "I hope" really isn't any different from "I wish." That's not the kind of hope the Bible talks about. You might hope you win the lottery, but you don't have any reason to believe you actually will. It's false hope. And that kind of hope doesn't really have any power to sustain you when times get hard.

> There is no situation so chaotic that God cannot from that situation, create something that is surpassingly good. He did it at the creation. He did it at the cross. He is doing it today.
>
> HANDLEY C. G. MOULE

The hope described in the Bible has more to do with confidence than with wishing. Hope is a conviction that you are moving toward a future that a good God holds in his hands. It's a belief that there is a reason for everything in your life, even if you don't understand the reason at the time. It's a confidence that all things—the sorrows no less than the joys—ultimately work for your good, your eternal happiness.

Your hope is as certain as Jesus Christ himself. The Bible speaks of "Christ in you, the hope of glory" (Colossians 1:27 KJV). Is Christ in you? Then you have hope, a hope to live for.

Sometimes life's sharp edges poke you where you feel the most tender. Sometimes you feel self-conscious or ugly or left out. But you have hope—real hope. That hope that God offers to his people is more than a vague wish that the sun will come out tomorrow; it's a genuine confidence that in all things, even these painful things, God is perfecting you, straightening you out, shaping you into something beautiful for all eternity.

> O Israel, hope in the Lord! For with the Lord there is steadfast love, and with him is great power to redeem.
>
> Psalm 130:7 NRSV

do something

You have a big future ahead of you. God has begun a good work in you, and he is going to complete it. Someday, when he is finished, you will look like Christ himself. In the meantime, let that hope shape every decision you make. Let that confidence control the way you think about yourself and the world around you.

hope · hope · hope · hope · hope · hope

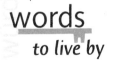

words
to live by

The Orthodontic Gospel

➤ Hope is a key component of good mental health. The human psyche needs to have good things to look forward to. Hopelessness, on the other hand, is a defining symptom of depression and a number of other mental health problems.

➤ In 1981, millionaire Eugene Lang gave a speech to the sixth graders at his old elementary school, which had a twenty-five percent graduation rate. Lang made them an offer: If they finished high school, he would help them pay for college. With that hope, ninety percent of them ended up graduating.

Be ready at all times to answer anyone who asks you to explain the hope you have in you.
1 Peter 3:15 GNT

Hope is not the conviction that something will turn out well, but the certainty that something makes sense regardless of how it turns out.
BARBARA JOHNSON

final thought

God, thanks to you I have hope—not just for this life, but for eternity too. Christ in me is the hope of glory. All praise to the One who is my hope. Amen.

hu·mil·i·ty, noun

1. a disposition to be humble; a lack of false pride.
2. freedom from pride and arrogance; lowliness of mind.
3. a modest estimate of one's own worth.
4. **Biblical:** a Christ-like willingness to lay aside one's own honor or dignity for the sake of another.
5. **Personal:** the ability to forget about yourself.

Beneath Your Dignity?

Humble yourselves before the
Lord, and he will exalt you.
James 4:10 NRSV

Who has the most important job at a swimming pool? That's an easy one: the lifeguards. The chirp of a lifeguard's whistle commands respect. Without the constant vigilance of lifeguards, a place of carefree summer fun could be a place of danger. Through training and ability, the lifeguards have earned the right to sit in the high seat. But at many pools, the lifeguards' duties go beyond keeping a watchful eye and making the occasional daring rescue. When a kid throws up in the pool, who cleans it up? The lifeguards. Who collects the trash and carries it to the Dumpster when everybody else goes home for the day? The lifeguards. Who scrubs the toilets in the changing rooms? In many cases, it's the lifeguards.

The truth is, much of a lifeguard's time is spent doing tasks that would seem to be "beneath" a person with such an important

words
to live by

job. That's what humility is all about: being able to forget about yourself—your glory, your standing, the recognition you think you deserve—roll up your sleeves, and do what needs to be done in every situation. Being humble means being willing to clean up a mess, even if you didn't make it. Sometimes it means being able to say you're sorry. Mostly, it means being able to step over the barriers that pride puts between people.

> God has two dwellings: one in heaven, and the other in a meek and thankful heart.
> **IZAAK WALTON**

Humility isn't low self-esteem. Being humble doesn't mean feeling untalented or worthless. As a matter of fact, true humility probably isn't possible for a person who feels insecure. Nor could you be very humble if your self-worth is tied up in what other people think about you. You might end up arrogant, you might end up self-pitying (and you'd probably end up a combination of the two), but you wouldn't end up humble.

The perfect example of humility, not surprisingly, is Jesus. He is God in his very nature, and yet on earth he was able to let go of the rights, the privileges, the honor that was due him. He took the form of a human being, and the eternal God allowed himself to die—not a peaceful death at a ripe old age, but a painful, shameful death. It was grim work. It was truly beneath him, to come in and clean up the mess that human beings had made of themselves. Yet he did it willingly. When you think on that, it's not so easy to convince yourself that you're too good to apologize, or too good to stoop down and serve.

Your dignity can be a huge stumbling block. Your pride can keep you from enjoying the abundant life Jesus promises to those who are willing to forget themselves long enough to grab hold of it. The gospel frees you from the need to be appreciated by the people around you. It frees you from the need to assert yourself, to sit in the front seat every time. You might as well face it: The world probably won't give you as much credit as you deserve. But when you feel disrespected, remember this one truth of the gospel: God gives you far more credit than you could ever deserve. He looks at you and sees the perfection of Christ. Understand that, and you can hardly help but be humble.

Humility comes before honor.
Proverbs 15:33
GOD'S WORD

do something

The great enemy of humility is the belief that you're not getting as much credit as you deserve. It's human nature: When you're right, or better, or quicker, or richer, you want everybody to acknowledge it. When you're wrong, when you lose, when you make a mistake, you hope nobody notices. Humility sets you free from all that.

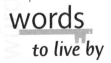

words
to live by

Don't push your way to the front; don't sweet-talk your way to the top. Put yourself aside, and help others get ahead. Don't be obsessed with getting your own advantage. Forget yourselves long enough to lend a helping hand.

Philippians 2:3–4
THE MESSAGE

He that is down need fear no fall, he that is low no pride.

JOHN BUNYAN

The Greek writer Xenophon used the picture of a horse under rein to explain true meekness or humility. A reined horse isn't weak. It's incredibly strong and powerful. But that power is under control. It doesn't constantly exert itself, but allows itself to be guided by the master. That's humility.

The innards of a deer used to be called *numbles*. A pie made of them was called "a numble pie," which became "an umble pie." "Eating umble pie" came to signify being publicly humiliated. Nowadays, numble pies are long forgotten, but everybody knows about "eating humble pie."

final thought

God, I think too much of myself. I waste a lot of energy making sure people give me the credit I think I deserve. Deliver me from that neediness, and give me the grace to rest in the knowledge that you thought enough of me die for me. Amen.

i·dol·a·try, noun

1. the religious worship of images that are not God.
2. excessive or blind adoration, reverence, or devotion.
3. *Biblical:* the worship of any created thing instead of the Creator.
4. *Personal:* the habit of placing your hope in anything besides God.

No Other Gods

Since we are God's offspring, we ought not to think that the deity is like gold, or silver, or stone, an image formed by the art and imagination of mortals.

Acts 17:29 NRSV

You're strolling through the mall when something you've never seen before catches your eye. There, next to the soft pretzel stand, somebody has set up a big statue of a calf. At the base of the statue is a plaque: FOR YOUR WORSHIPING CONVENIENCE. Somebody is promoting idolatry right there in the mall. Would you bow down and worship? Probably not. It just seems so primitive. Idolatry, like witchcraft or pagan fertility rituals, is one of those sins you read about in the Bible and think, *Well, there's one I can check off my list.* Chances are, your friends aren't carving out statues and praying to them either.

Not so fast. You don't have to bow to a carved statue to worship an idol. Idolatry is putting any created thing where God ought to be. It is God who makes you what you are. Your worth—every bit of it—is derived from God. Not from accomplishments. Not from

words
to live by

money. Not from clothes. Not from your carefully cultivated tastes in music. Not from popularity or influence. Not from any created thing. And frankly, that can be hard to swallow. Because you have some control over created things. You can make more money. You can achieve more accomplishments. You can buy new clothes. Idolatry is as simple as putting your trust in things you have some control over.

Whenever we take what God has done and put it in the place of himself, we become idolaters.

OSWALD CHAMBERS

The prophet Isaiah made fun of the idolaters of his time. An idolater will cut down a tree that God has caused to grow, that God has watered with the rain. Half of the tree they throw onto a fire to warm themselves and make bread. But the other half they carve into an idol. They bow down to it and worship it. They pray to it, saying "Save me; you are my god" (Isaiah 44:17 NIV).

It seems ridiculous. But it happens every day. God gives good gifts, and people turn to those gifts, not to the Giver, and say "Save me." They may not say "You are my god," but they look to the gift to do what only God can do. They look to money to make them feel secure. They look to success to make them feel worthy. They look to a boyfriend or girlfriend to make them feel loved.

The cure for idolatry begins with a simple statement: God is God, and nothing else is. It's easy to understand, but it's not always easy to accept. God isn't under your control. But that's

i·dol·a·try·i·dol·a·try

a good thing. It's human nature to make gods who are a little more manageable than the true God. However, a god that you can manage is a god that can't do much for you. God is all-powerful. God is all-knowing. And God is good. He will meet your needs—even needs you didn't know you had—and lead you on to glory. Trust in him. Worship him. Thank him for his gifts. And never let those gifts take his place in your heart.

> You shall have no other gods before me. You shall not make for yourself an idol in the form of anything in heaven above or on the earth beneath or in the waters below. You shall not bow down to them or worship them.
>
> Exodus 20:3–5 NIV

do something

How about you? Are you looking to any created thing to meet a need that only God can meet? There are probably idols in your life. What needs have you been looking to them to fulfill? You can be sure that God, the one and only true God, meets those needs more completely—and more permanently—than any idol could.

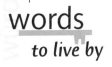

words
to live by

The word of the LORD came to me, saying, "Son of man, these men have set up their idols in their hearts and have put right before their faces the stumbling block of their iniquity. Should I be consulted by them at all?"
Ezekiel 14:2–3 NASB

Idolatry: trusting people, possessions, and positions to do what only God can do.
BILL GOTHARD

᠁ When Paul visited Athens, he was struck by the huge number of idols and altars he saw. There was even an altar labeled "to an unknown god." Afraid of accidentally offending any left-out god, the Greeks made this general-purpose altar just to be on the safe side.

᠁ In the late 1500s, a Japanese warlord named Hideyoshi commissioned an enormous statue of Buddha. Soon after the statue was completed, an earthquake destroyed it. Furious, he shot an arrow at the idol, shouting, "I put you here at great expense, and you can't even look after your own temple."

Final thought

God, there are no other gods before you. But sometimes I forget, and I make idols of things I can see and touch—things I can control to some extent. Forgive me, and give me a heart to serve the one true God. Amen.

joy • joy • joy • joy • joy • joy • joy • joy • joy

graciousness peace humble holiness obey repent perfect submit
serve fellowship comforter transformed noble character church

joy, noun

1. the emotion of great delight or happiness.
2. a source or cause of keen pleasure or delight.
3. the expression or display of gladness.
4. **Biblical:** a deep delight experienced by believing Christians.
5. **Personal:** the unshakeable sense of well-being, security, and happiness that comes from being in the presence of God.

and the Pursuit of Joy

Let all who take refuge in you be
glad, let them ever sing for joy.
Psalm 5:11 NASB

Remember studying the Declaration of Independence in history class? One of the most memorable and most quoted passages from that great document states that all people have a God-given right to "life, liberty, and the pursuit of happiness." The pursuit of happiness—what could be more American than that? It's what brings immigrants from all over the world to America—the hope not only of pursuing happiness here, but of finding it. It's what motivated millions of people to go west in search of a better life.

Yet there's something more important than the pursuit of happiness: the pursuit of joy. Does that sound like the same thing? It's not, actually. Happiness always depends on what happens to you. To pursue happiness is to put yourself in a position where good things will happen. Joy, on the other hand, goes much deeper. Joy is a feeling of well-being, of security—call it happiness

words
to live by

if you like—that stays alive no matter what your circumstances. Genuine joy is a response not to what is happening around you, but to what God is doing in your life.

"In Your presence is fullness of joy; at Your right hand are pleasures forevermore" (Psalm 16:11 NKJV). In a sense, the pursuit of joy isn't a pursuit at all. It's a stillness, a willingness to sit in God's presence and rejoice in him. There is some happiness to be found in the things of earth, and there's not necessarily anything wrong with pursuing that kind of earthly happiness. But the genuine joy that comes from knowing God is worth so much more. If you're pursuing happiness, you'd better be ready to keep moving. Circumstances change. A friend moves away. You blow a test. A romance fizzles. So you keep on chasing. Joy isn't a promise that those sad or disappointing things won't happen in your life. Rather, it's a promise that the God who fills your life to overflowing will continue to bless you even in those times.

The best argument for Christianity is Christians: their joy, their certainty, their completeness. But the strongest argument against Christianity is also Christians—when they are somber and joyless, when they are self-righteous and smug in complacent consecration, when they are narrow and repressive, then Christianity dies a thousand deaths.

SHELDON VANAUKEN

Joy isn't just an add-on to the Christian faith. It's one of the central facts of a life that's lived for Christ. Jesus compared the kingdom of heaven to a treasure that a man finds hidden in a field: "And from joy over it he goes and sells all that he has and buys that field" (Matthew 13:44 NASB). This man, this God-seeker, is willing to sell out everything—every hope of earthly happiness he ever had—so he can get his hands on a greater treasure. And what's his motivation? Joy. It's not a bad trade: mere earthly happiness for the joy of heaven. The incredible thing is that once you've made the trade, you get earthly happiness back again. Joy isn't just something to look forward to. It's something you can have right now.

Godly joy is a recognition that God is your all in all, the sum of all your desires. But even more than that, joy is the realization that this God is yours. In his right hand are pleasures forever, and he reaches that hand out to you.

> Rejoice in the Lord always; again I will say, Rejoice.
> **Philippians 4:4** NRSV

do something

Happiness can be found in a lot of different places. The problem is, once you've found happiness, you can't count on it to stick around. What you really want is joy. Joy can be found in only one place. But that place isn't hard to get to. Joy is found in God's presence; and as you learn to delight more and more in the presence of God, you're getting a head start on the unshakable joys of heaven.

> Philippians is the apostle Paul's joy book. In this tiny epistle (just four short chapters), the words *rejoice* and *joy* appear nineteen times. Paul was bursting with joy as he wrote—and yet he was imprisoned as he wrote this book, probably chained to a Roman guard.

> David danced in the streets when the Ark of the Covenant was returned to Jerusalem. He danced so wildly and so joyously that his wife, Michal, scolded him for his undignified behavior. David refused to be chastened. "It was before the Lord," he answered. "I will celebrate before the Lord."

I have told you this so that you will be as joyful as I am, and your joy will be complete.
John 15:11 GOD'S WORD

Oh, the fullness, pleasure, sheer excitement of knowing God on Earth! I care not if I never raise my voice again for Him, if only I may love Him, please Him.
JIM ELLIOT

 **final thought**

God, don't let me be satisfied with anything less than the joy of being in your presence. Protect me from anything that might lure me away from that simple joy. Amen.

king·dom of God, noun

1. the spiritual realm of which God is the acknowledged king; sometimes called the *kingdom of heaven.*
2. the authority or dominion of God.
3. *Biblical:* the reign of God, not only in heaven, but on earth as well.
4. *Personal:* God's authority in the hearts and lives of his people.

Territory

Your kingdom come, your will be done on earth as it is in heaven.
Matthew 6:10 NIV

In 1940, German tanks rumbled down the broad avenues of Paris. France had fallen to the Nazis, and the future looked grim—not just for France, but for all of Europe. But in the face of such ruthless, seemingly unstoppable power, a secret network of freedom-loving French men and women began to form in cafés, farmhouses, and apartment buildings throughout France. In whispered conversations in half-lit rooms, they laid plans to oppose the invaders and pave the way for the return of legitimate government in their country. They were the French Resistance, some of the most beloved heroes of World War II.

The French Resistance never bowed the knee to the invader, never recognized the Nazis as France's rulers. To them, France was still France. It would never be just another province of Germany's empire. They longed for the day when their nation

words
to live by

would be restored to its former glory. In the war's darkest hours, that hope kept them going.

Every time you pray "thy kingdom come," you're a little bit like a member of the French Resistance. That prayer expresses a longing for the day when the kingdom of God will break through in such a way that no one can deny that God rules on earth just as he does in heaven. It's a forward-looking view of God's kingdom. And yet

> Wherever God rules over the human heart as King, there is the kingdom of God established.
>
> **PAUL W. HARRISON**

Jesus, who taught his disciples to pray "thy kingdom come," also said, "the kingdom of God is in your midst" (Luke 17:21 NASB). In other words, Jesus taught his followers to long for the kingdom of God while at the same time teaching them that the kingdom of God has come already. How could that be?

Planet earth is occupied territory. Satan has set himself up as the authority, in opposition to God, its rightful ruler. This foreign power demands your obedience. And yet this is still God's world. When he became a human being, lived here, died here, and rose again from the dead, he renewed his claim on this world. And sometime in the future, he will come again to establish his kingdom once and for all. Meanwhile, where does your allegiance lie? Consider the French Resistance. They loved their country, even though it couldn't have seemed much like their country when the Nazis were in charge. And they kept the French spirit alive in spite of their conquerors. Every time they protected a Jewish family from the Nazis' evil laws, the

French Resistance reasserted the values of their freedom-loving nation. The flame flickered, but it never died out. Eventually, the Nazis were overthrown, and the warming fires of freedom burned again. France was France once more.

The kingdom of God is here, and yet it isn't here in its fullness. The kingdom asserts itself every time one of God's people serves another in the name of Christ. It asserts itself every time one of God's people does what's right instead of what's easy, every time God's people gather together to worship. The kingdom of God is in your midst now, but it isn't yet what it will be. In the now, only those who follow Christ understand that he reigns on earth. But the day will come when everyone will know, and God's people will have their reward in full.

"Turn away from your sins," [John the Baptist] said, "because the Kingdom of heaven is near!"

Matthew 3:2 GNT

do something

The re-invasion of earth is in the works, and you're part of the advance team, preparing the way. Every time you obey God's law of love instead of Satan's laws of selfishness and greed, you make the world look a little more like the kingdom of God. So don't grow weary in doing good. The kingdom is coming.

words
to live by

He has rescued us from the one who rules in the kingdom of darkness, and he has brought us into the Kingdom of his dear Son.
Colossians 1:13 NLT

The kingdom of God is a kingdom of paradox, where through the ugly defeat of a cross, a holy God is utterly glorified. Victory comes through defeat; healing through brokenness; finding self through losing self.
CHARLES W. COLSON

In the time of Christ, a group called the Zealots sought to establish the kingdom of God through violence. They urged rebellion against the Romans, believing that a warrior-Messiah would rise up and lead them in battle. They weren't looking for a Messiah who preached turning the other cheek.

William Wilberforce brought the kingdom of God to bear on the kingdom of England. A committed Christian and member of the British Parliament, he introduced an antislavery bill every year from 1788 to 1806. After eighteen years, the bill finally passed.

final thought

God, I eagerly wait for the day when everybody will know, in heaven and on earth, and underneath the earth, that Jesus Christ is Lord. May your kingdom come, and may your will be done here on earth, just as it is in heaven. Amen.

lib·er·ty, noun

1. freedom from despotic government or rule.
2. freedom from bondage, captivity, or physical restraint.
3. freedom from external control or interference, obligation; freedom to choose.
4. *Biblical:* freedom from the bondage of sin and the bondage of man-made rules.
5. *Personal:* freedom to do what is right.

You will know the truth, and
the truth will set you free.
John 8:32 GNT

You've just turned sixteen. You finally have your driver's license. Title, registration, and insurance are all in order. You're driving just below the speed limit. You're perfectly legal. It's a good feeling. You're free to go wherever you like. Want to drive to a friend's house? Go ahead—that's what a driver's license is for. Want to go to the mall? Drive on. Wave at the policeman with the radar gun. You've got nothing to fear.

True liberty exists within certain limits. The rules of the road don't limit a driver's liberty; they preserve it. Stay within the limits of the law, and your car gives you tremendous freedom. Step outside those limits, and your freedom will be restricted. At the very least, the freedom of your conscience will be compromised, your heart jumping into your throat every time you see a police car. At worst, you may have an accident. You don't have much

words
to live by

liberty when your car is smashed and you're laid up in the hospital.

God's rules, like the rules of the road, are not intended to destroy freedom, but to protect it. Within the boundaries of God's law, Christians have great freedom. It is sometimes the tendency among religious people, however, to impose extra rules and laws on themselves and others—rules that didn't come from God. They make one-size-fits-all rules about how long a person's hair should be, what kind of music a person should listen to, how often a person should have a quiet time. The message of the gospel is liberty. Christ came to people who were burdened down with rules, and declared, "[God] has sent me to proclaim release to the captives" (Luke 4:18 NASB).

> There are two freedoms—the false, where a man is free to do what he likes; the true, where a man is free to do what he ought.
> CHARLES KINGSLEY

That's why the apostle Paul was so upset when he found out his friends at the Galatian church were adding extra rules to the gospel he had preached to them. "So Christ has really set us free," he wrote. "Now make sure that you stay free, and don't get tied up again in slavery to the law." (Galatians 5:1 NLT). He had offered them freedom in Christ, but as soon as his back was turned, they took the chains of legalism back on themselves. A little later, however, he warned them not to go to the opposite extreme and abuse their freedom: "For you have been called to live in freedom—not freedom to satisfy your sinful nature, but freedom to serve one another in love" (Galatians 5:13-14 NLT). So what's the result of living in that kind of liberty? The fruits of the Spirit are free to grow in your life: "When the Holy Spirit controls our lives, he will produce this kind of fruit in us: love, joy, peace, patience, kindness, goodness, faithfulness, gentleness, and self-control. Here there is no conflict with the law" (Galatians 5:22-23 NLT).

The boundaries still exist, but within those boundaries, God calls you to liberty, not more and more rules. It's tempting to follow extra human-made rules "just to be on the safe side." But the Bible rejects that attitude. Liberty isn't optional for a Christian; it's the very basis of your holiness.

> Through Christ Jesus the law of the Spirit of life set me free from the law of sin and death.
> **Romans 8:2** NIV

do something

Liberty isn't just more fun than being enslaved to human-made rules. It also makes you a better servant of God. If you're depending on a list of rules to show you how to serve God, you're not depending on the Holy Spirit. The Christian faith is full of paradoxes, and Christian liberty is one of the biggest: When you throw out human-made rules and embrace freedom, you become a better servant of God.

words
to live by

Once when Martin Luther had explained the grace and freedom offered in the gospel, a shocked listener said, "If this is true, a person could simply live as he pleased!" Luther answered, "Indeed. Now, what pleases you?"

Before becoming a Christian, Saint Augustine reveled in the twisting complexities of philosophies and theories. After he came to Christ, he reveled in the simplicity of the gospel. He boiled Christian liberty into a single short sentence: "Love God, and do as you please."

God purchased you at a high price. Don't be enslaved by the world.
I Corinthians 7:23 NLT

The basic test of freedom is perhaps less in what we are free to do than in what we are free not to do.
ERIC HOFFER

final thought

God, you have set me free. Guide me in that freedom, and guard me from the temptation to throw that freedom away by letting myself be enslaved again to laws and rules that don't come from you. Amen.

Sweet Freedom

love, noun

1. a feeling of warm personal attachment or deep affection, as for a parent, child, or friend.
2. a profoundly tender, passionate affection for a person of the opposite sex.
3. a strong predilection or liking for anything.
4. *Biblical:* God's tenderness toward his people.
5. *Personal:* the impelling force that causes a person to look and act like Jesus.

Dear friends, we must love each other because love comes from God. Everyone who loves has been born from God and knows God. The person who doesn't love doesn't know God, because God is love.

I John 4:7–8 GOD'S WORD

In the movie *About a Boy*, the main character is an incredibly self-centered man named Will. Meaningful relationships are completely absent from his life, and that's the way he wants it. He has no family. He lives alone. He has a few friends he goes out with in the evenings, but they don't really know him that well. He doesn't even have work friends; he's so rich he doesn't need to work, so he mostly just hangs around his apartment figuring out ways to amuse himself.

Will's isolation ends when a young teenage boy named Marcus elbows his way into Will's life. Marcus is needy in many ways. He's fatherless, and his mother is too consumed with her own problems to give him what he needs emotionally. Marcus's ragged, off-brand clothes are a sharp contrast to Will's stylish dress. His socially awkward manner cramps Will's bachelor-suave

words
to live by

style. His emotional neediness is confusing and distressing to a man who thinks he's never needed anything.

But in the end the boy breaks through, and Will realizes that he does indeed need other people. In the movie's climactic scene, Marcus has entered his school talent show as part of a desperate attempt to make his depressed mother happy. He's singing her favorite song, a sappy love ballad from the 1970s, and it's painful to watch. He has no musical accompaniment, no singing ability, no stage presence. His classmates, who have never been kind to Marcus anyway, nearly boo him off the stage.

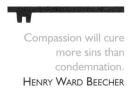

Compassion will cure more sins than condemnation.
HENRY WARD BEECHER

Then something wonderful happens: Will slips onstage from the wings and stands behind Marcus. He has a guitar in his hands, but his playing is only slightly better than Marcus's singing. Still, he's there to back up his young friend, helping to absorb the abuse and humiliation that Marcus's classmates heap on him. That's a great picture of love in action. Will, who has never cared about anything but his own comfort, his own dignity, willingly allows himself to be pelted with rotten fruits and vegetables, willingly bears insults that aren't even his to bear. And it's the first thing that's made him happy in a long time.

That scene illustrates a couple of things about the nature of love. First, genuine love causes you to look and act like Jesus. Standing up for Marcus, carrying his burden, taking his friend's shame on himself, Will made a sacrifice that resembled (in a much smaller way) the sacrifice that Jesus made. When you love someone, you are willing to lay aside your interests for the interests of another person (John 15:13; Ephesians 5:25). Secondly, Will's act of love on the talent show stage illustrates the fact that love is an act of the will, and not just a feeling. It's interesting that in the definitions quoted above, the three taken from regular dictionaries all describe love in terms of feelings or affections. That's the world's view of love: a warm, fuzzy feeling. Good feelings are definitely one aspect of love. But any love that's worth its salt results in actions, and loving actions require an act of the will. Will made a decision to join Marcus on the talent show stage.

> By this all will know that you are My disciples, if you have love for one another.
> John 13:35 NKJV

Believers love others because God loved them first. And the result is people who look more and more like Jesus.

do something

Love is more than a feeling; it's a commandment. "This is My commandment," said Jesus, "that you love one another, just as I have loved you" (John 15:12 NASB). In the previous verse, Jesus said he's giving these commandments so that his followers' joy may be made full. It's one of the many paradoxes of Jesus' teachings: When you forget about your own happiness long enough to think about somebody else's, your joy is made full.

words
to live by

There are three things that will endure—faith, hope, and love—and the greatest of these is love.

1 Corinthians 13:13 NLT

I have found the paradox that if I love until it hurts, then there is no hurt, but only more love.

MOTHER TERESA

There are two main Greek verbs for love—*agapao* and *phileo*. *Agapao* portrays love as an act of will. *Phileo* has more to do with affectionate feelings. It's worth noting that everywhere God commands you to love, the word is *agapao*, love as an act of will, not as a feeling.

C. S. Lewis offered this advice: "Do not waste time bothering whether you 'love' your neighbour; act as if you did. As soon as we do this we find one of the great secrets. When you are behaving as if you loved someone, you will presently come to love him."

final thought

God, you have loved me beyond my wildest dreams. Make me shine like a mirror to reflect that love to those around me—that my joy may be full. Amen.

mer·cy, noun

1. compassionate or kindly forbearance shown toward an offender, an enemy, or other person in one's power.
2. the disposition to be merciful.
3. an act of kindness, compassion, or favor.
4. **Biblical:** God's compassion toward his people.
5. **Personal:** a habit of kindness; a habit of forgiveness.

Be merciful, just as your
Father is merciful.
Luke 6:36 NIV

Think of a friendless person at your school. Every school has a few. They float somewhere outside the circle of activity, unnoticed, uncared for. They may not look quite right. Sometimes they smell bad. Their people skills are often nonexistent. Now, think what it would be like to be a friend to that person. It might be costly. It certainly wouldn't improve your social standing to be seen hanging with such an outsider. And you can be sure it would be a lot of aggravation. When you're a person's only friend, things can get messy and over-involved pretty fast.

But if you managed to hang tough and be a friend to the friendless, you would be performing an act of mercy. To be merciful is to reach out and give to a person who has nothing to give back to you. Befriending the head cheerleader would not be an act of mercy. Mercy is a willingness to relieve the sufferings of those

words
to live by

who have been taking a beating from life: widows, the fatherless, the poor, the bereaved, the friendless, prisoners, and other people who are down and out.

Another aspect of mercy is closely related to forgiveness and grace. When you have the power to punish a wrongdoer and choose not to, you are exercising mercy. You may not often find yourself in a position to dish out punishment, but you do find yourself in a position to forgive. An unmerciful heart finds it hard to forgive and prefers to hold a wrongdoer hostage instead.

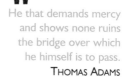

He that demands mercy and shows none ruins the bridge over which he himself is to pass.

THOMAS ADAMS

What's the connection between these two aspects of mercy—kindness to the suffering and forgiveness to the guilty? They both come down to how you treat people who are less powerful than you. You exercise a certain amount of power over a person who has wronged you. How you use that power— either mercifully or unmercifully—says a lot about your character. Likewise, you only have to see a bully making a weakling beg for mercy on the playground to see what an unmerciful heart looks like.

Mercy is the basis of God's interaction with his people. You've heard the saying, "God helps those who help themselves." But in fact, the Gospel says just the opposite: God helps those who cannot help themselves. He redeems his own not because they show promise, not because he needs them on his team, not because he owes it to them, but simply because "He delights in mercy" (Micah 7:18 NKJV). He forgives the same sins over and over again, no matter how many times his people abuse his forgiveness and slide back to their old ways. Why? Because he delights in mercy. He comforts the afflicted. He is a Father to the fatherless. Why? Because he delights in mercy.

> The steadfast love of the Lord never ceases, his mercies never come to an end; they are new every morning; great is your faithfulness.
> **Lamentations 3:22–23** NRSV

You are called to be like God, to be his image-bearer in the world. If his relationships with human beings are seasoned with mercy, so should yours be. "Be merciful, just as your Father is merciful" (Luke 6:36 NIV).

do something

God has been merciful to you. His blessings have never been based on what you could do for him; they have always been based on his sheer loving-kindness. In the same way, it is your privilege and duty to show mercy to those around you. This is true godliness. There's no better way to show the world what God is like.

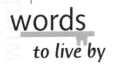

words
to live by

Have you ever wondered how "saying uncle" came to be a way of begging for mercy? The phrase may have started with Irish immigrants to America. The Irish word *anacol* means "mercy," but it sounds a lot like "uncle" (especially when somebody is twisting your arm behind your back).

The top of the Ark of the Covenant was called the Mercy Seat. Once a year, one of the High Priests would enter the Holy of Holies to meet with God in front of the Mercy Seat. God's interactions with his people began and ended with mercy.

Your own soul is nourished when you are kind, but you destroy yourself when you are cruel.

Proverbs 11:17 NLT

Upon you I call, O God, my mercy, who made me and did not forget me when I forgot you.

SAINT AUGUSTINE OF HIPPO

final thought

God, your mercies are new every morning. But still I sometimes withhold mercy from those people around me who need it most. Use me, God, to show others what your mercy looks like. Amen.

Have Mercy

o·be·di·ence, noun

1. the act or state of being submissive to the restraint or command of authority.
2. dutiful compliance.
3. to follow the guidance of.
4. **Biblical:** the fulfillment of God's claims or commands.
5. **Personal:** the habit of submitting your own will to the will of God.

Be Done

Be obedient to God, and do not allow your lives to be shaped by those desires you had when you were still ignorant.

I Peter 1:14 GNT

Here's a question: Can you be who God wants you to be, and still be who you want to be? Don't answer too quickly. It's not supposed to be an obvious answer. The question could be put another way: Do you truly believe that God has a better plan for you than you have for yourself? The whole matter of obedience comes down to that one question.

Your desires and hopes sometimes come into conflict with God's requirements. You need to make a good grade on a test, for instance. You *really* need to, or else your grade point average will suffer, and if you don't have a good grade point average you won't be able to get into the kind of college you want to go to. The test in question would be very easy to cheat on. Everybody else seems to be cheating on it, and besides, if the teacher didn't want you cheating, she should make it harder to cheat. But on the other

words
to live by

hand, you know that cheating is wrong, and that God forbids it. You're faced with a choice: Do you follow your own agenda, in which a good grade is the key to your future happiness, or do you follow God's agenda, which places more importance on your integrity than on your grade point average?

Of course, questions of obedience aren't usually as dramatic as that. They aren't usually about your long-term life plan coming into conflict with God's long-term plan. More often, the conflict revolves around what you feel like doing at one particular moment—a thought you feel like dwelling on, a Web site you feel like visiting, an urge you feel like acting on. But the principle is still the same. Your will comes into conflict with God's will. Your idea of happiness doesn't match up with God's plan to make you eternally happy, and you have to make a decision.

Cowardice asks the question, "Is it safe?" Expedience asks the question, "Is it political?" Vanity asks, "Is it popular?" But conscience asks the question, "Is it right?" There comes a time when one must take a position that's neither safe, nor political, nor popular, but he must make it because his conscience tells him that it's right.
MARTIN LUTHER KING JR.

Even Jesus, God made flesh, experienced that conflict. The night before he was to suffer an agonizing death on the cross, he prayed that God might spare him such suffering and redeem humanity some other way. "Father," he said, "if you will, take this cup of suffering away from me. Not my will, however, but your will be done" (Luke 22:42 GNT). There's an obedient heart summed up in a single sentence: "Not my will, however, but your will be done." The desire of Jesus to avoid the intense suffering of the cross is understandable. He was made of flesh, after all. But he also understood that the desires and hopes of his flesh were very small next to God's eternal purposes for him—and for all humanity through him.

So can you be who God wants you to be and still be who you want to be? That depends on what you want. If your motto is "my will be done," you don't want nearly enough. But if you can pray with an obedient heart, "not my will but yours be done," you can be sure you will be everything you ever hoped you would be—and much, much more.

> Thanks be to God that though you were slaves of sin, you became obedient from the heart to that form of teaching to which you were committed.
> **Romans 6:17** NASB

do something

Obedience happens moment by moment. It's fine to say, "I'm going to be obedient from here on out." An overall commitment to obedience is a great starting place. But remember, your will exerts itself constantly—all day, every day. You have to be on constant guard. Keep submitting your will to the will of God, moment by moment.

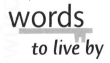

words
to live by

Christians have always struggled with the balance between grace and obedience. One of the extreme positions in that debate is called antinomianism. Antinomianism is a false doctrine that says that obedience isn't necessary. Since God is gracious and forgiving, an antinomian would say, you don't have to bother with obedience.

Samuel said: "Has the LORD as great delight in burnt offerings and sacrifices, as in obeying the voice of the LORD? Behold, to obey is better than sacrifice."
I Samuel 15:22 NKJV

Only he who believes is obedient. Only he who is obedient, believes.
DIETRICH BONHOEFFER

Are you ever tempted to disobey because a particular command seems too small to bother with? Horatius Bonar put that attitude in perspective: "It is not the importance of the thing, but the importance of the Lawgiver that is to be the standard of obedience."

Final thought

God, I know that your plan is better than mine. When I am tempted to disobey, when I secretly suspect that my plan is better than yours, help me to remember that your will is perfect. Amen.

pa·tience, noun

1. the bearing of provocation, annoyance, misfortune, or pain without complaint, loss of temper, or irritation.
2. the ability or willingness to suppress annoyance when confronted with delay.
3. quiet perseverance.
4. **Biblical:** the ability to stand firm in spite of disappointment or hardship.
5. **Personal:** the ability, when things don't go according to your plan or schedule, to trust that God's plan for the situation is better.

straining at the leash

I waited patiently for the Lord's help;
then he listened to me and heard my cry.

Psalm 40:1 GNT

Have you ever seen a young dog out for a walk with its owner, the dog straining against the leash at every step? Never quite happy with the master's pace or choice of route, it nearly chokes itself lunging this way and that. But the master's pace never changes. For all its straining, the dog doesn't get where it's going any faster. It's just more exhausted when it gets there.

You don't see so many old dogs straining at the leash. They lope along enjoying the scenery, sniffing at the occasional tree, barking at the occasional squirrel. They don't wear themselves out trying to lunge ahead. They've learned that they're better off going at their owner's pace, saving their energy, enjoying the walk, taking it as it comes. They've learned to trust that their owner is going to get them where they need to be. Impatience grows from a mistaken belief that you should have control over

words
to live by

things that you just can't control—the passage of time, for instance, or traffic jams or little sisters. Impatience is straining against the leash as if that might get you where you want to be faster; but you only wear yourself out and make yourself miserable trying to hurry things that can't be hurried.

It takes five to seven minutes to cook a frozen pizza. That's just the way it is. You can stare hungrily at the oven all you want. You can drum your fingers impatiently on the counter. But it won't make the pizza cook any faster. Of course, you could also pull the pizza out after a minute or two, but only if you aren't bothered by a patch of ice in the middle of a pizza topped by unmelted strips of mozzarella. Good things—liked fully cooked pizza—come to those who wait.

> The most extraordinary thing about the oyster is this: irritations get into his shell. . . . And when he cannot get rid of them, he uses the irritations to do the loveliest thing an oyster ever has the chance to do. If there are irritations in our lives today, there is only prescription: make a pearl. . . . And it takes faith and love to do it.
> **HARRY EMERSON FOSDICK**

Impatience is a good way to make yourself miserable. Refusing to accept things that you cannot change only wears you out. The real problem with impatience, however, is that it's a form of unbelief. The impatient heart says (though maybe not consciously) "If I were in charge of the universe, I think I'd run a tighter ship." A patient heart is a trusting heart. It accepts and rests in the fact that God is good and his plan is perfect, whether you understand the plan or not.

"But those who wait for the Lord shall renew their strength, they shall mount up with wings like eagles, they shall run and not be weary, they shall walk and not faint" (Isaiah 40:31 NRSV). God is good to those who are able to wait for him, to trust in him. He gives them a quiet kind of strength that keeps them going long after the childish outbursts of impatience have exhausted themselves. Wait patiently for the Lord. His timing is perfect.

> Patient endurance is what you need now, so you will continue to do God's will. Then you will receive all that he has promised.
>
> **Hebrews 10:36** NLT

do something

It's one thing to say you believe that God's plan is perfect in a general sense. The key to patience, however, is to trust that God's plan is perfect in this particular situation—in the situation where you're tired of waiting, or confused about the way things are working out, or annoyed with the person ahead of you in the drive-through line.

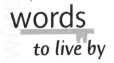

words
to live by

Let us not become weary in doing good, for at the proper time we will reap a harvest if we do not give up.
Galatians 6:9 NIV

This hard place in which you perhaps find yourself is the very place in which God is giving you opportunity to look only to Him, to spend time in prayer, and to learn long-suffering, gentleness, meekness—in short, to learn the depths of the love that Christ Himself has poured out on all of us.
ELISABETH ELLIOT

It seems strange, but all the Greek words for *patience* used in the New Testament were originally military terms. They call up images of soldiers enduring under enemy attack. In the battles of life, the Christian bears up bravely, like a soldier.

The California poppy is a picture of patience. Once its seeds are scattered, the seeds lie dormant on the floor of the desert waiting for the next abundant rains. Sometimes they wait for years. But as soon as the rains come, the seeds spring to life, starting the flower's life cycle again.

Final thought

God, I know your timing is perfect. And yet it's hard to wait. Strengthen me. Help me to trust in your wisdom, your goodness—today, in this situation. In every situation. Amen.

Straining at the Leash

peace, noun

1. the normal, nonwarring condition of a nation, a group of nations, or the world.
2. cessation of or freedom from any strife or dissension.
3. freedom of the mind from annoyance, distraction.
4. **Biblical:** a state of blessed harmony resulting from a spiritual completeness.
5. **Personal:** a state of inner rest and calm.

smile in the Storm

Therefore, having been justified by faith, we have peace with God through our Lord Jesus Christ.

Romans 5:1 NKJV

The first evening of a voyage across the Atlantic, one of the passengers—a preacher—stood up at dinner and announced that he would be leading a prayer meeting at six o'clock each morning for the duration of the voyage. All passengers and crew were invited to join him. The next morning, however, the preacher prayed alone. Nobody made it out of their bunks to join him. At dinner that night, the preacher repeated his announcement, but again nobody came the next morning. It went on like that for several days, the preacher praying alone while everybody slept.

Late one night, however, the ship ran into a storm—one of those howling, rocking, sideways-raining storms that ravage the North Atlantic. Through the wee hours of the morning, the huge ship pitched and tilted on the swelling sea like a toy boat in a bathtub. Everyone was terrified—passengers and crew alike. At six

words
to live by

o'clock, the storm still howling, the cabin appointed for the prayer meeting was packed. Everyone on board, it seemed, had squeezed into the little room to pray for deliverance. But the preacher was nowhere to be found. Somebody ran to his cabin. No preacher. A few of the braver souls set out in the wind and rain to look for him.

They found him on the ship's deck. He was holding tight to a railing and grinning into the ocean spray that blew up from the rolling water. "Reverend!" one of the search party shouted over the howling wind. "It's time for prayer meeting!"

"Go ahead without me," the preacher called back. "I've been praying all week. This morning, I'm just going to enjoy this display of God's power."

> How completely satisfying to turn from our limitations to a God who has none. . . . For Him time does not pass, it remains. . . . God never hurries. There are no deadlines against which He must work. To know this is to quiet our spirits and relax our nerves.
> **A. W. TOZER**

God promises to give you peace—permanent peace, the kind that surpasses all understanding. He does not, however, promise to put you in permanently peaceful situations. Anybody can feel peaceful when the sky is blue, the sea is calm, and they're making good progress toward their destination. But the preacher facing down the storm had peace on the inside—even when the situation around him was in chaos—because he trusted in the God who had even that storm under control.

Psalm 23 is probably the best-loved picture of peace in all the world. "The Lord is my shepherd, I shall not want." Sheep in green pastures, beside the still waters—what better image of peace than that? But sheep aren't always in green pastures, not even in Psalm 23. Sometimes they're in the valley of the shadow of death. But even then they enjoy the peace that comes from being in the Good Shepherd's care: "Even though I walk through the valley of the shadow of death, I will fear no evil, for you are with me" (Psalm 23:4 NIV). You might know the camp song that says, "With Jesus in the boat you can smile in the storm." That's the kind of peace God offers: not permanent blue skies, but the ability to smile in the storm, secure in the love and protection of the Prince of Peace, who always leads his people safely home.

> The mind set on the flesh is death, but the mind set on the Spirit is life and peace.
> **Romans 8:6** NASB

do something

True peace is the ability to have inner calm when the circumstances around you are stressful or otherwise chaotic. But you probably shouldn't wait for the most stressful times in your life to start practicing the peace of Christ. Pray regularly and feed on God's word in the normal, comparatively peaceful times of life. Then, when things get hairy—finals week, for example—you can fall back on habits of peace.

words
to live by

But now in Christ Jesus you who once were far off have been brought near by the blood of Christ. For he is our peace.

Ephesians 2:13–14 NRSV

The fierce grip of panic need not immobilize you. God knows no limitation when it comes to deliverance. Admit your fear. Commit it to Him. Dump the pressure on Him. He can handle it.

CHARLES SWINDOLL

Shalom (or *salom*, the Hebrew word for *peace*, is the standard "hello" and "good-bye" for Hebrew-speaking people. The same word is the root for the city-name *Jerusalem*. It means literally "foundation of peace."

Researchers have estimated the number of peaceful years the world has known since the beginning of recorded history. World peace has very much been the exception rather than the rule. In the last four thousand years, there have been fewer than three hundred years that the world has been free from war.

final thought

God, reign in my heart. When life's storms rage, only you can give me peace. And when my circumstances are calm, I pray that you will give me your peace then too. Amen.

per·se·ver·ance, noun

1. steady persistence in a course of action, a purpose, or a state.
2. steadfastness; doggedness.
3. to persist despite opposition or obstacles.
4. *Biblical:* resistance, steadfastness under pressure, and endurance in the face of trials.
5. *Personal:* the determination to keep on keeping on.

Run for Your Life

We must run the race that lies ahead of us and never give up. We must focus on Jesus, the source and goal of our faith.
Hebrews 12:1–2 GOD'S WORD

Sports Illustrated called Ben Comen the slowest high-school cross-country runner in America. He has never finished better than last in a race. When the other runners—even most of the slow ones—are crossing the finish line, Ben is just getting to the halfway point. And yet he has become a hero and a source of inspiration not only in his hometown of Anderson, South Carolina, but for sports fans throughout the country.

Ben has cerebral palsy, which makes it extremely difficult to walk, much less run. Nevertheless, he runs 3.1 miles every race, struggling with every step. A cross-country course isn't smooth and flat like a stadium track. There are hills and dips, rocks and branches in the path. Even those little obstacles can be a big problem for a person with cerebral palsy. He falls a lot, and he falls flat, because his hands don't get the message to catch him. Time and

words
to live by

time again he picks himself up, battered and bloody, and keeps going.

But in spite of all that, Ben has never failed to finish a race. He keeps plodding along, never concerned that the other runners have finished the race before he reaches the halfway mark. He's not racing against them anyway. He's racing against his own unique challenges. "I like to show people that you can either stop trying or you can pick yourself up and keep on going," he says. "It's just more fun to keep on going."

> Great works are performed not by strength but by perseverance.
> **Samuel Johnson**

It's that attitude that has made Ben a hero among his teammates. After they have finished, they go find him on the course and run the last part of the race with him. In fact, runners from other teams join in too, and when Ben crosses the finish line, he's often followed by dozens of runners in different uniforms cheering him on and inspiring him to keep running, just as he has inspired them. And the crowd goes wild.

Hebrews 12:1 compares the life of faith to a race: "Let us throw off everything that hinders and the sin that so easily entangles, and let us run with perseverance the race marked out for us" (NIV). Sometimes it seems easier just to quit. You fall down. You get bruised and bloodied. You feel you just don't have what it takes to run this race, especially when you see others for whom everything seems so easy. But it was God who marked this race out for you, and it is God who gives you the strength to persevere.

The key to perseverance is to focus on the finish line, not on the difficulties of the moment that make you feel like quitting. "Let us fix our eyes on Jesus, the author and perfecter of our faith, who for the joy set before him endured the cross, scorning its shame, and sat down at the right hand of the throne of God" (Hebrews 12:2 NIV). What kept Jesus going? The joy that was set before him.

The same joy is set before you. It's waiting at the finish line, where you'll sit at the throne of God. So keep on keeping on. As Ben Comen put it, "It's just more fun to keep going."

> If you abide in My word, you are My disciples indeed.
>
> **John 8:31** NKJV

do something

Do you ever feel you weren't cut out for a life of Christian faith? Do you feel like you're falling down more than you're running? Are you ever afraid that the latest failure is the last straw? Keep pressing on. You're not running in your own strength anyway. God has begun a good work in you, and he's going to see it through to perfection.

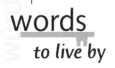

words
to live by

The missionary William Carey once said his best quality was an ability to plod along. "I can plod. I can persevere in any definite pursuit." He knew about perseverance. He worked as a missionary in Burma for seven years before he saw the first person converted to Christ.

In protest over Charles Simeon's appointment as pastor, the members of Trinity Church locked the pews; anyone who wanted to hear Simeon preach had to sit or stand in the aisles. But Simeon's perseverance won over the members; he pastored the church for fifty-four years.

Staying with it—that's what God requires. Stay with it to the end. You won't be sorry, and you'll be saved.
Matthew 24:13
THE MESSAGE

The pilgrim who spends all his time counting his steps will make little progress.
BISHOP JEAN-PIERRE CAMUS

 final thought

God, it's hard to keep pressing on. Still, I know that it was you who marked out this course for me. And you can give me the strength to keep going. Amen.

pow·er, noun

1. the ability to do or act; capability of doing or accomplishing something.
2. strength; might; force.
3. the possession of control or command over others; authority.
4. **Biblical:** the authority and strength of God to exercise his will.
5. **Personal:** God's strength made real in the life of the believer.

A Real Power Trip

> When we brought you the Good News, it was not only with words but also with power, for the Holy Spirit gave you full assurance that what we said was true.
>
> **1 Thessalonians 1:5** NLT

In 1990, Michael Jordan was at the height of his career with the Chicago Bulls. Many nights it seemed he could score at will; nothing could stop him. On March 28 of that year, in a playoff game against the Cleveland Cavaliers, he scored an amazing, career-high sixty-nine points. Even for a very good NBA player, that would be more than enough points for two great games. The same night, a rookie named Stacey King got some playing time for the Bulls. He scored one point, a single free throw. After the game, King gave reporters his own take on Michael Jordan's big night: "I'll never forget," he joked, "the night Michael Jordan and I combined for seventy points!"

When the power of God is at work in your life, you feel a little bit like Stacey King. You and God combine to do incredible things—to overcome sin, to love the unlovable, to bring people to

words
to live by

Christ. Meanwhile, all you've done is hit one or two free throws. Consider Romans 16:20: "The God of peace will soon crush Satan under your feet" (NASB). It's God who's going to crush Satan, but he's going to use your feet to do the crushing. It may not be your power, but still it's got to be a good feeling to have the prince of darkness, the author of destruction, underneath your boot heel.

In human terms, what does it mean to be a powerful person? It means you get your way. That's all anybody really wants, isn't it? To be in a position where nobody can force you to do anything you don't want to do. In one sense at least, power means the exact same thing in a biblical context. God is the ultimately powerful One. He always does as he pleases. That's what people mean, really, when they speak of God's power.

> Each of us may be sure that if God sends us on stony paths He will provide us with strong shoes, and He will not send us out on any journey for which He does not equip us well.
> **ALEXANDER MACLAREN**

But what about you? What kind of power do you have through God? You now have the power to do as you please. You have the power to overcome the world. Does that sound exaggerated? It's not. As you line up your will, your desires with the will of God, you find that you have the power to overcome any force that might try to bend you to its will.

Apart from Christ, the world will defeat you. Sure, you might be able to win according to the rules that the world has put into place. You can be the most popular person at your school without Christ. People do it all the time. You can make the best grades. You can get rich. But any power you get from that kind of success is only an illusion. In the end, it melts away. The power of God in your life isn't the world's kind of power. It's the power to live your own life, free from the sin that tries to enslave you. It's the power to crush Satan underneath your feet. How's that for a power trip?

> In the world you will have tribulation; but be of good cheer, I have overcome the world.
>
> **John 16:33** NKJV

do something

God has lots of ways to exercise his power on earth. You can see it in nature, in a thunderstorm, or in the movement of the stars. Every now and then he displays his power in miracles. Another of the ways God exercises his power is through his people—through people like you. Are you ready to be used by God?

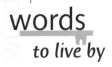

words
to live by

All riches and wealth come from you; you rule everything by your strength and power; and you are able to make anyone great and strong.

1 Chronicles 29:12 GNT

"Safe?" said Mr. Beaver . . . "Who said anything about safe? 'Course he isn't safe, but he's good. He's the King, I tell you."

C. S. LEWIS

◦ The New Testament word for *power* is *dunamos*, as in "dynamite." That helps put the idea of spiritual power in perspective. It's not just a vague idea or feeling. The power of God in a believer's life is explosive.

◦ One of the most vivid expressions of Jesus' power was the power to heal. In one instance, a woman who had been sick for seven years merely touched the hem of his cloak and was healed when power went out from Jesus into her.

final thought

God, as you display your power, as you crush Satan, I pray that you would see fit to use me. Make me ready to be an instrument of your power. Amen.

praise, noun

1. the act of expressing approval or admiration.
2. the offering of grateful homage in words or song.
3. the state of being admired or approved.
4. **Biblical:** the act of speaking well of God, often in song or psalm.
5. **Personal:** a celebration of excellence, especially the excellence of God.

Yum! Yum! Good!

Enter his gates with a song of thanksgiving. Come into his courtyards with a song of praise. Give thanks to him; praise his name.

Psalm 100:4 GOD'S WORD

You're sitting at dinner, and much to your delight, your favorite dessert is being served. You take one bite and realize that it's not just your favorite dessert; it's the most perfect example of your favorite dessert you've ever eaten. It just melts in your mouth. There's one thing you can be sure of: You won't sit there quietly. Something is going to come out of your mouth—"Yum, that's good," or "Ooh, you've got to try this." You will praise that dessert, and you won't even have to think about it.

You were made to praise. You can't help it. When you really enjoy something, praise bubbles up spontaneously. If you're a basketball fan, you can't help but cheer when you see a jump shot arc from the top of the key and swish home, nothing but net. The truth is, you might even have to restrain yourself from a quick little cheer when the other team makes a shot that beautiful. Skill,

words
to live by

beauty, excellence, love—all these things inspire praise.

Why do you praise? One reason is to compliment the person who made the dessert or the jump shot. But that's not the chief reason you break into sponta- neous praise. Think about it: you can be eating by yourself, but if you get a taste of something really good, you're still going to say "Yum." It just comes out. In fact, you might even be more effusive in your praise of a sparerib if there's nobody around to hear you (or to see the barbecue sauce on your face). When you're watching a game on television, you still cheer a great play, even though the players you're cheering can't enjoy your compliment.

With Jesus' help, let us continually offer our sacrifice of praise to God by proclaiming the glory of his name.
Hebrews 13:15 NLT

As C. S. Lewis pointed out, you praise because praise com- pletes your enjoyment of the thing or person being praised. You haven't fully enjoyed the beauty of a sunset until you say (if only to yourself) "Wow, that was beautiful," or something similar. If your praise of a thing makes somebody feel appreci- ated or complimented, so much the better. That's a happy by- product of spontaneous praise. But it's not the main point.

There are lots of places in the Bible where God commands people to praise him. That seems strange, doesn't it? Is God saying "Compliment me, flatter me, massage my ego"? Of course not. God doesn't need an ego boost. When he invites you to praise him, it's so that your pleasure—your enjoyment of him—will be increased, not so he'll feel better about himself.

The praise of God is the natural outpouring of a heart that loves God. Think about how you feel when you've got a new boyfriend or girlfriend. You feel like telling that person how great he or she is. For that matter, you feel like telling everybody else how great your boyfriend or girlfriend is too (though, hopefully, you resist the urge). It's the same with God. If you're in love with God, you feel like talking about how great he is. You feel like singing songs of praise. If you love God, all those commands to praise him are just commands to do what comes naturally.

Let everything that breathes praise the Lord! Praise the Lord!
Psalm 150:6 NRSV

do something

When you're in a right relationship with God, praise is the natural result. But it works the other way around too. Sometimes the feelings result from the praise. When you're not feeling very close to God, and praise doesn't seem natural, praise God anyway; meditate on the words of praise found in the Psalms. That's a good way to get yourself to a place where your relationship can be restored.

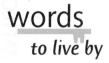

words
to live by

O LORD, You are my God. I will exalt You, I will praise Your name, for You have done wonderful things; Your counsels of old are faithfulness and truth.
Isaiah 25:1 NKJV

Be not afraid of saying too much in the praises of God; all the danger is of saying too little.
MATTHEW HENRY

The Hebrew word for "praise" is *halal*. From this root comes the word *hallelujah*. The word *hallelujah* has gone worldwide, breaking down language barriers everywhere. The word "hallelujah," according to *Vine's Bible Dictionary*, "has been taken over into virtually every language of mankind."

The book of Psalms is truly rich in praise. The word *praise* (or some version of it) appears 187 times in the Psalms. That's 1.25 praises per psalm. The prize of most "praises" per verse goes to Psalm 150—thirteen "praises" in six verses.

 final thought

God, you are my God, and I will praise you forever. Keep me in a place where the praise of God comes as naturally to my lips as praise of the things of earth. Amen.

prayer, noun

1. a devout petition to, or any form of spiritual communion with, God.
2. a formula or sequence of words used in or appointed for praying; the *Lord's Prayer*.
3. a petition; entreaty.
4. **Biblical:** communication with God; the offering to him of petitions, thanksgiving, and praise.
5. **Personal:** a habit of turning every thought toward God.

Thinking God's Thoughts

Ask, and it will be given you; search,
and you will find; knock, and the
door will be opened for you.

Matthew 7:7 NRSV

The Bible says to "pray without ceasing" (1 Thessalonians 5:17 KJV). Some translations say "pray continually" or "pray all the time." That's fine, but how are you supposed to get anything done if you're praying all the time? You'd get pretty hungry if you spent your entire lunch hour asking the blessing instead of eating lunch. And the boss at your after-school job probably wouldn't appreciate it if you spent your entire shift with head bowed and eyes closed while customers were waiting to be served. Obviously, Paul was talking about some other way of praying.

People tend to think of prayer as an event—an activity you can check off your list of things to do for the day, or a ritual you do before meals, or something you blurt out almost involuntarily when you're in trouble. Is prayer on your to-do list? If so, good; scheduling a time of quiet reflection is a vital part of a healthy

words
to live by

prayer life. But you should also be aware that a morning quiet time is just the tip of the iceberg when it comes to obeying the command to pray without ceasing. Instead of thinking about prayer as a task you can check off your to-do list, it might be more helpful to think of prayer as a house to be lived in. Prayer is a state of being, a communion with God that doesn't require that you sit still and close your eyes.

When the Bible talks about praying without ceasing, it's really talking about a habit of thinking "God-ward." In other words, every thought that enters your mind lifts you up toward God—his plan, his pleasure, his values. To pray without ceasing is to recognize that you are

> I have been driven many times to my knees by the overwhelming conviction that I had nowhere else to go. My own wisdom, and that of all about me, seemed insufficient for the day.
>
> **ABRAHAM LINCOLN**

enveloped by the eternal—that God is as close as the air you breathe. Prayer reaches through everyday chaos to grab hold of the peace and rest of God's eternity. Prayer brings the eternal to bear on the things of the world, so that you see the eternal significance of everything in your life. A passing thought about a flower's beauty becomes an occasion to praise the God who created it. Every worry—big and little—is lifted from your shoulders and carried off into the safekeeping of God who never fails. A flash of anger or bitterness or lust is transformed into a moment of dependence on the God who is forever molding you into the image of Christ. Your hopes and dreams are no longer idle wishes, but prayers presented before the throne of the God who delights to give you the desires of your heart.

The point of prayer isn't to change God's mind—to persuade him to give you what you want. The point is to change *your* mind. As you pray without ceasing, your thoughts begin to look more like God's thoughts. Your hopes begin to look more like God's will. And "in Jesus' name" is no longer just a phrase tagged on for a little extra prayer insurance. It becomes the hallmark of your life.

> You can ask for anything in my name, and I will do it, because the work of the Son brings glory to the Father. Yes, ask anything in my name, and I will do it!
> **John 14:13–14** NLT

do something

What does it mean to pray "in Jesus' name"? It means you pray for what Jesus would pray for if he were praying. Of course, you don't always know what Jesus would pray in every situation; that's why some prayers appear to go unanswered. But it's a comfort to know that when you don't always know what to pray for, the Holy Spirit is praying on your behalf (Romans 8:26).

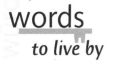

words
to live by

You will seek Me and find Me, when you search for Me with all your heart.
Jeremiah 29:13 NKJV

Be still, and in the quiet moments, listen to the voice of your heavenly Father. His words can renew your spirit. No one knows you and your needs like He does.
JANET L. WEAVER

A prayer offered up in a time of emergency by a person who doesn't normally pray is sometimes called "a foxhole prayer." The phrase originated with soldiers in battlefield foxholes, where they often were forced to wait out barrages of enemy fire. Many soldiers prayed their first prayers in foxholes.

William Temple, a man of prayer, spoke often of the prayers that God answered in his life. A critic once told him that what he called answered prayers were actually just coincidences. Temple answered, "When I pray, coincidences happen; when I don't, they don't."

Final thought

God, awaken in me the desire to pray without ceasing. Change my mind, so that I can think your thoughts after you and confidently pray. Amen.

pride, noun

1. the state of thinking well of oneself as the result of accomplishments or possessions.
2. self-respect.
3. arrogant behavior or conduct.
4. **Biblical:** the sin of thinking too highly of oneself.
5. **Personal:** self-reliance in matters where only God is reliable.

Slip-Up

A Royal

See that man who thinks he's so smart? You can expect far more from a fool than from him.

Proverbs 26:12 THE MESSAGE

Hezekiah is remembered as one of the good kings of Old Testament Judah. He abolished the idol worship that had flourished in the reigns of his predecessors. He shored up the kingdom's defenses and ensured Jerusalem's water supply—no small feat in that dry land. As a result of Hezekiah's faithfulness, God richly blessed the whole kingdom with peace and prosperity throughout his reign. But even good King Hezekiah was susceptible to pride, and one small slip-up proved costly for Judah.

If anyone ever had reason to trust in God rather than his own strength and ability, it was Hezekiah. Time and again, God delivered him in impossible situations. Once, the Assyrians, the world's most powerful and ferocious army, camped outside Jerusalem, preparing to overrun the city. Judah was in no shape to defend itself against such an enemy. So Hezekiah prayed for deliverance.

words
to live by

pride • pride • pride • pride • pride • pride

God delivered his people in a spectacular way. The next morning, the bodies of 185,000 Assyrian soldiers lay scattered around the camp, having mysteriously died in the night. The remaining Assyrians were understandably creeped out. They broke camp and went home as soon as possible. Word spread quickly about the little kingdom that had put the mighty Assyrians to flight, and nobody messed with Judah for the remainder of Hezekiah's reign.

Hezekiah was miraculously delivered another time. He was gravely ill, lying on his deathbed. Even the prophet Isaiah had

The national anthem of hell is "I Did It My Way."
PETER KREEFT

dropped by to tell him he wouldn't survive the illness. But Hezekiah prayed for healing, just as he had prayed for deliverance from the Assyrians. Once again God did a miracle. Hezekiah was healed.

That's when Hezekiah slipped up and was guilty of pride. The king of Babylon sent ambassadors to Jerusalem to congratulate Hezekiah on his recovery. Hezekiah was no doubt feeling a little exuberant. His health was back, and his kingdom was prosperous. So he took the Babylonian ambassadors on a tour of all his storehouses. They saw all the silver and gold, all the spices and oils, all the arms and armor. Maybe Hezekiah just felt like showing off. Or maybe his little guided tour was an effort to intimidate the Babylonians by showing them how wealthy and powerful he was. In any case, Hezekiah's display had the opposite effect. It just demonstrated to the Babylonians that Jerusalem would be a rich prize for their growing empire. Eventually, the Babylonians destroyed Jerusalem and carried the people of Judah into slavery.

That's pride in a nutshell. God gives blessing after blessing, and then somewhere along the way you start to believe that you deserve credit for the blessings. You pray for deliverance from the Assyrians, and then when you've been delivered, pride whispers in your ear, "Check you out—you just defeated the Assyrians."

The real problem with pride isn't just that you go around bragging, as obnoxious as that is. The real danger is that pride convinces you to transfer your faith from God to your own gifts and abilities. Pride talks you into showing off your strength, but, as Hezekiah found out, you end up showing off your vulnerabilities.

> Do not think of yourself more highly than you should. Instead, be modest in your thinking, and judge yourself according to the amount of faith that God has given you.
> **Romans 12:3** GNT

do something

The surest cure for pride is not to think more poorly of yourself, but rather to think more highly of God. Every ability, every gift, every good thing you have comes from God—including the things you feel you've earned. Enjoy those gifts. But steer clear of the trap of believing you can trust those gifts rather than the Giver.

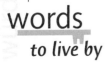

words
to live by

O LORD, my heart is not proud, nor my eyes haughty; nor do I involve myself in great matters, or in things too difficult for me.
Psalm 131:1 NASB

You can have no greater sign of a confirmed pride than when you think you're humble enough.
WILLIAM LAW

The Seven Deadly Sins, according to early Christian theologians, are pride, sloth, gluttony, lust, greed, anger, and envy. No matter whose list you look at, the same sin is always at the top of the list: pride. It is pride that gives rise to all the other sins.

Peacocks have a reputation for being excessively proud of their beautiful plumage. But according to ancient legends, they were also ashamed of their feet, which didn't fit in with their otherwise splendid appearance. They supposedly shrieked with embarrassment every time they caught sight of their feet.

final thought

God, you are the source of all the good things in my life. Deliver me from the danger of relying on myself in situations where only you are reliable. Amen.

pri·or·i·ty, noun

1. the state of being earlier in time, occurrence.
2. precedence in order, rank, or privilege.
3. precedence in obtaining certain supplies or services.
4. **Biblical:** the importance one attaches to a goal, activity, or task.
5. **Personal:** where your heart is.

First Things First

I want you to understand what really matters, so that you may live pure and blameless lives until Christ returns.

Philippians 1:10 NLT

You've got a cup of sand, a cup of marbles, and six golf balls. Your task is to fit all that—sand, marbles, golf balls—into a mayonnaise jar. But there's a problem: A cup of sand plus a cup of marbles makes two cups—half the jar's capacity. And six golf balls by themselves fill the jar well past the halfway mark. Simple math tells you it's impossible to fit everything in the jar, doesn't it? Actually, no. There's a trick. First you put in the golf balls. Then you pour in the marbles, shaking the jar so the marbles fit into the space between the golf balls. Then you pour in the sand, which settles in the spaces between the marbles. Do it the other way around—first sand, then marbles, then golf balls—and you'll have a problem. You'll find yourself trying to fit six golf balls in half a mayonnaise jar, and it won't work. If you take care of the little stuff first, you'll find there's not enough room for the big stuff.

words
to live by

Your life is like that mayonnaise jar. You can only fit so much in. But if you're smart about it and take care of the big, important things, you'll be surprised how much you can squeeze in.

Jesus said the same thing in another way: "Seek first the kingdom of God and His righteousness, and all these things shall be added to you" (Matthew 6:33 NKJV). Once you get your priorities straight—once you promote the things of God to the top of your to-do list—you'll find room for everything else you need to do. True, certain things will get squeezed out of your life. There are only twenty-four hours in a day, after all. But if you're putting God first, what do you think is going to get squeezed out? All the stuff that wastes your time and drags you down. There's more than enough time for what really matters—family, friends, church, schoolwork, rest and relaxation, hobbies—you can make your own list.

> It is impossible to do everything people want you to do. You have just enough time to do God's will. If you can't get it all done, it means you're trying to do more than God intended for you to do (or, possibly, that you're watching too much television).
> RICK WARREN

If you're not paying attention, the little things—things you know don't matter very much—will fill up so much of your jar that you won't have space left over for the big things. You sit and watch one extra hour of television or play one more video game, so you get in bed an hour later than usual. Next morning, you can't quite make it out of bed for a quiet time before school the way you had planned. You can always do it after school. But after school you find yourself looking at a friend's really cool Web site, which links off to some Web sites that are actually kind of boring, but you don't feel like getting up. Then it's dinnertime, and after dinner you've got schoolwork that just has to get done, but you're so far behind now that you have to stay up two hours past bedtime to get it all done. And the next morning, your quiet time is really out of the question.

First things first. Seek the kingdom of God. Don't worry, you won't miss out on anything important. You might miss some television or a few boring Web sites. But all the really good stuff, God will add that to you.

> He himself is before all things, and in him all things hold together.
> **Colossians 1:17** NRSV

do something

If you want to get your priorities straight, you have to take control of your schedule. Fortunately, there's a magic word for that very purpose. If you can learn to use this magic word properly, your life will be lined up with your priorities in no time. Here it is: 'no.' You can regain control of your life by saying no to those activities that don't match up with your priorities.

words
to live by

In the 1930s, a man offered Charles Schwab a productivity technique: list the things you need to do tomorrow; number them by importance; order your day accordingly. He told Schwab to try it, then pay him whatever he thought the advice was worth. Schwab sent the man $25,000.

Thomas Jefferson's epitaph, which he wrote himself, reveals his priorities. It reads, "Here was buried Thomas Jefferson, author of the Declaration of American Independence, of the Statute of Virginia for Religious Freedom, and Father of the University of Virginia." He didn't mention that he was President of the United States.

Seek first his kingdom and his righteousness, and all these things will be given to you as well.
Matthew 6:33 NIV

Taking first things first often reduces the most complex human problem to a manageable proportion.
DWIGHT EISENHOWER

Final thought

God, give me the wisdom to see the difference between the important and the merely urgent, and the character to pursue only that which is important. Amen.

unless grace mercy love faith devote [...]
[...]iveness peace humble holiness obey repent perfect submit
[...]ve fellowship comforter transformed noble character church

pur·pose, noun

1. the reason for which something exists or happens.
2. an intended or desired result.
3. determination; resoluteness.
4. **Biblical:** God's plan for a person's life; the reason for which God created each person.
5. **Personal:** the goal toward which you are striving.

What Are You Doing Here?

"For I know the plans I have for you," declares the LORD, "plans to prosper you and not to harm you, plans to give you hope and a future."
Jeremiah 29:11 NIV

In Greek mythology, a figure named Sisyphus was condemned to roll a huge boulder up a hill in Hades for all eternity. It's his specially designed torture. He works and strains, grunts and groans to get the humongous rock up the hill. Then, when he has almost made it to the top, he loses his grip and has to watch it tumble all the way to the bottom of the hill. Down he goes after it. When he gets to the bottom, he puts his shoulder to the boulder and starts the whole thing over again. Up the hill an inch at a time, down the hill in a few sickening seconds. Up the hill, down the hill. Over and over for all eternity. Sisyphus could hardly suffer a more miserable fate. It's not just the exhaustion. It's the purposelessness. He works and works, and there's just no point in it. In spite of his efforts, the boulder always finds its way to the bottom.

Sisyphus provides a chilling picture of a life without purpose.

words
to live by

He's not idle. He works. He stays busy. But all that activity isn't directed toward any meaningful purpose. If your purpose—the things you're living for, the goals you're striving for—doesn't reach beyond the things of this world, your efforts will lack eternal purpose. You won't ever get the boulder to the top of the hill.

James Dobson tells a story about playing Monopoly with his family. As the game progressed, he got more and more absorbed in the world of the game, buying property, charging rent, passing Go, collecting two hundred dollars. He had a sense of purpose: to build his little empire, to run his opponents into bankruptcy. He won the game. But his sense of achievement was short-lived. As he folded up the board and put away the paper money, he was struck by the emptiness of his victory, the purposelessness of his consuming purpose that evening. From the perspective of eternity, the strivings of earth seem as temporary and minor as a Monopoly game. The board will be folded up, the paper money stashed away, and all that's left will be the things you did with a view to eternity.

> A saint's life is in the hands of God as a bow and arrow in the hands of an archer. God is aiming at something the saint cannot see; He stretches and strains, and every now and again the saint says, "I cannot stand any more." But God does not heed; He goes on stretching until His purpose is in sight, then He lets fly.
>
> **OSWALD CHAMBERS**

So what is your purpose? What exactly are you doing here? You are here to know Christ. More specifically, you are here to begin knowing Christ, in preparation for an eternity of dwelling in his presence. The apostle Paul said he considered everything to be loss compared to the surpassing greatness of knowing Christ. The hope of that fuller knowledge was what kept him going through discouragement, failure, difficulty; it's what gave his life purpose. "Not that I have already obtained it or have already become perfect, but I press on so that I may lay hold of that for which also I was laid hold of by Christ Jesus" (Philippians 3:12 NASB). Run to win the prize that Christ has already won for you. How's that for certainty of purpose?

> The human mind may devise many plans, but it is the purpose of the Lord that will be established.
>
> **Proverbs 19:21** NRSV

do something

You were made for a purpose. You didn't just appear. God had a good reason for putting you here, for making you the person he made you, for placing you in the situations he's put you in—even when it seems that surely something has gone wrong with God's plan. And this purpose is eternal; it doesn't suddenly become irrelevant when life's game board is folded up.

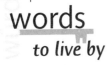

words
to live by

I cry out to God Most High, to God who will fulfill his purpose for me.
Psalm 57:2 NLT

When you become consumed by God's call on your life, everything will take on new meaning and significance. You will begin to see every facet of your life—including your pain—as a means through which God can work to bring others to Himself.
CHARLES STANLEY

There used to be a popular bumper sticker that read, "He who dies with the most toys, wins." James Dobson proposed an alternative version that has more truth in it: "He who dies with the most toys, dies anyway."

Catcher Yogi Berra chattered to distract opposing batters. Once when Hank Aaron was hitting, Berra suggested that he adjust his grip to read the bat's trademark. But Aaron cracked a home run and then turned to Berra: "I didn't come up here to read."

final thought

God, give me strength to keep striving to win the goal you have already won for me: the knowledge of Christ. Amen.

re·pent·ance, noun

1. remorse or contrition for a wrongdoing, or the like.
2. regret for past action.
3. the act of changing for the better as a result of remorse or contrition for one's sins.
4. *Biblical:* a change of mind or heart that results in more godly conduct.
5. *Personal:* a radical change in your motivations.

Turn This Thing Around

Change your life. Turn to God and be baptized, each of you, in the name of Jesus Christ, so your sins are forgiven. Receive the gift of the Holy Spirit.

Acts 2:38–39 THE MESSAGE

Repentance is all about changing directions. You're headed in one direction, a bad direction, and then you come to your senses, modify your course, and head off in a better direction. It seems easy enough: Just put forth a little effort, straighten up, and fly right—right? Well, not exactly. There's more to repentance than just making up your mind to work harder at being good. To repent is to make a change that's deeper than a change in behavior. It's deeper even than a change in attitude or outlook. To repent is to stop being motivated by your human nature and start being motivated by the Spirit.

Picture yourself on a big cruise ship. You're out for a stroll on the deck when you notice that you're heading straight for an iceberg. What do you do? You could turn tail and run toward the back of the ship. Instead of walking east, you'd be running west. That's

words
to live by

a complete change of direction, right? Wrong. Running westward on an eastbound ship isn't going to accomplish very much. The whole ship has to change directions.

By nature, you live by the flesh. That means you go after the things that your human nature wants: power, pleasure, selfishness, etc. It also means you try to solve your problems by the means that are available to the flesh. If you can, you try to buy your way out of trouble or talk your way out. Or maybe you do decide to work harder to do what's right. That's better than cheating or stealing, but if your

> To move across from one sort of person to another is the essence of repentance: the liar becomes truthful, the thief, honest.
> **A. W. TOZER**

efforts at self-improvement aren't powered by the Spirit, you're just running west on an eastbound ship. It's only a matter of time before your human nature collides with real trouble.

The problem is, you always end up doing what you want to do. And your human nature wants the wrong things. You might know in your head what's right and what's wrong. You might even know in your head that doing right works out better in the end than doing wrong. But if you're relying on your own flesh, you're eventually going to give in to what your flesh wants.

So how do you get the ship turned around? You begin walking by the Spirit. "Let the Spirit direct your lives, and you will not satisfy the desires of the human nature" (Galatians 5:16 GNT). That's repentance: to stop being motivated by your human nature and start being motivated by the Spirit. If you are in Christ, you have a new self. That self wants what the Spirit wants. But your old self is still hanging around too. And that old self is always looking for a chance to elbow its way in and exert its will. It's a struggle you'll deal with constantly as long as you're on this side of heaven. That's why repentance is a daily thing: not turning once to Christ, but surrendering every day to the Holy Spirit who lives within you, asking not only for the strength to do what's right, but also right desires that overcome the desires of your human nature.

> No one who conceals transgressions will prosper, but one who confesses and forsakes them will obtain mercy.
> Proverbs 28:13 NRSV

do something

You may be tempted to think that because you do things that are wrong, you must not really want to do what's right. Don't despair. If the Spirit lives in you, you're a new creation, with new desires. Unfortunately, you still have an old self that wants to do its own thing. Walk by the Spirit. And tell your old self to take a hike.

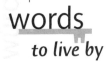

words
to live by

Godly sorrow produces repentance leading to salvation, not to be regretted; but the sorrow of the world produces death.

2 Corinthians 7:10 NKJV

Man is born with his face turned away from God. When he truly repents, he is turned right round toward God; he leaves his old life.

D. L. MOODY

◥ The New Testament word for *repentance* is *metanoia*. It literally means "a change of mind," but it encompasses more than just thinking new ideas. It's a change of mind that causes changes in the whole person.

◥ Regret isn't the same thing as repentance. People can feel regret or remorse, be sorry they got caught, even be genuinely ashamed of their behavior, yet still not change their ways. But when the Spirit is at work, conviction of sin leads to genuine and lasting change.

final thought

God, I want to walk by the Spirit, but my old self keeps taking over. Overpower that old self so that I will go after the desires of the Spirit. Amen.

res·ur·rec·tion, noun

1. the act of rising again from the dead.
2. the state of one who has returned to life.
3. the act of bringing back to practice, notice, or use; revival.
4. *Biblical:* the rising again of Christ from the dead.
5. *Personal:* new life, which begins when you are rescued from the deadness of sin.

He Is Risen (and So Are You)

He will take these weak mortal bodies of ours and change them into glorious bodies like his own, using the same mighty power that he will use to conquer everything, everywhere.

Philippians 3:21 NLT

The Sunday morning after Jesus was crucified, two women came to Jesus' tomb to tend to his body. But when they got there, the stone sealing the tomb entrance had been rolled away. Jesus' body wasn't there. The women jumped to the conclusion that someone had broken in and stolen the body. It was a reasonable enough assumption. A dead person can't just walk off under his own power. The women had thought Jesus would be their deliverer, but now that just looked like one more false hope. He was dead, and they didn't even have a body left to pay their respects to. After all the indignities Jesus had suffered, a grave robbery seemed like one more painful insult.

Then through their tears the women noticed two men they had never seen before, dressed in dazzlingly bright clothes. The men—they were angels, it turned out—asked a question that

words
to live by

changed everything: "Why do you seek the Living One among the dead?" It must have taken a moment or two before the women understood what the angels were telling them. "He is not here," the angels continued. "He is risen."

He is risen. That one fact means that Christianity isn't a mere belief system, the helpful teachings of a wise and good man. The Resurrection means that Christianity is the one and only path to eternal life. Jesus passed from death into life, and you can follow him there. The Resurrection shows that Jesus is Lord even over death.

The man in Christ rose again, not only the God. That is the whole point.
C. S. LEWIS

Resurrection is the cornerstone of the Christian faith. It's not just Jesus who came back to life, but everyone who believes in him. When Jesus lived on earth, people had a hard time staying dead anytime he was around. He brought back the little daughter of Jairus, the synagogue official, and the son of the widow of Nain. Lazarus had already begun to rot in his grave when Jesus brought him back to life. And so it will be with all the followers of Christ. They won't stay dead either.

In this fallen world, things seem always to be disintegrating, turning back into the dust from which they were made. Everything that lives is sliding toward death. People get sick, old, and decrepit. Not even young people are exempt from death. You might have had schoolmates who have died. But the God of the Resurrection will reverse all that. The old saying claims that nothing is certain but death and taxes. With the resurrected Christ, not even death is certain—or certainly not final.

If you are in Christ, the bodily resurrection of the dead is your future hope. If you are in Christ, you have experienced a resurrection already: "Even when we were dead in our transgressions, [God] made us alive together with Christ" (Ephesians 2:5 NASB). Dead people can't raise themselves. Dead people don't have much to offer. Nevertheless, God took hold of you in your spiritual disintegration, put the pieces back together, and breathed life into them. That's the miracle of the Resurrection at work in you.

> It is the will of him who sent me that I should not lose any of all those he has given me, but that I should raise them all to life on the last day.
>
> John 6:39 GNT

do something

You live in a world where things fall apart. But you serve a God who puts things back together. Sometimes it looks like death is in charge of things. You can't turn on the television without news of murders, bombings, wars. But Christ won the victory over death; he is leading you out of the valley of death and into eternal life.

words
to live by

If the Spirit of Him who raised Jesus from the dead dwells in you, He who raised Christ from the dead will also give life to your mortal bodies through His Spirit who dwells in you.

Romans 8:11 NKJV

Christ is alive and He will be alive forever! He has been alive and with His people all down the centuries! He is alive and with His people today; He will be alive and with His people to the end. Jesus Christ alive! He was in our yesterdays; He is in our todays; and thank God He will be in our tomorrows.

JOHN DANIEL JONES

A plant called the resurrection fern grows on the branches of big trees, mostly in the southeastern United States. When the weather is dry, this little fern turns brown and curls up as if dead. But when the rains come again, it "resurrects," turning full and green and healthy once more.

There were actually four other people besides Jesus who raised people from the dead in the Bible: Elijah and Elisha in the Old Testament, and Peter and Paul in the New. Of course, besides Jesus, none of them raised the dead in their own power.

Final thought

God, you have put life back into my dead spirit. I praise your name. And when my body dies, I won't stay dead. Hallelujah. Amen.

righ·teous·ness, noun

1. the quality or state of being characterized by uprightness of morality.
2. conduct that is morally right or justifiable.
3. a system of moral conduct.
4. **Biblical:** conformity to God's standards of perfection.
5. **Personal:** the state of being lined up with the will of God.

Your Spiritual Posture

God's way of putting people right
with himself has been revealed. . . .
God puts people right through
their faith in Jesus Christ.

Romans 3:21–22 GNT

"Sit up straight!" How many times have you heard that one? There's a reason your mom always insisted on good posture. When you stand or sit up straight, your whole body is in alignment. Your back and neck muscles aren't subjected to unnecessary strain. Your lungs and chest have more room to expand when you breathe. Your feet and legs feel better. And perhaps most important, good posture helps safeguard against back trouble and a permanent hunching when you get older. It's all about alignment. Keep yourself straight, and things work the way they're supposed to.

Righteousness is all about alignment too. It's a highly theological sounding word, but righteousness just means being lined up with God's values and attitudes. Righteousness is your spiritual posture. When you get a little slouchy, you start to feel the

words
to live by

strain all over. You don't breathe quite so freely. You start to feel spiritually fatigued. Righteousness isn't easy. Your spiritual spine isn't straight by nature. And even after God has intervened in your life to straighten you out, you still have a tendency to slump in your seat if you're not paying attention.

The real test of good posture is how you sit when you're at rest. Anybody can sit straight when there's somebody in their face yelling "Sit up straight!" The real question is, which feels more comfortable to you? Slumping like a potato sack or sitting with your back straight and shoulders squared? It's the same with righteousness. When there's nobody looking over your shoulder, do you feel more comfortable doing things that please God or just living like the world around you? Righteousness isn't just a matter of stringing together a few good deeds or making a few good decisions. Righteousness is a frame of mind—a habit of the heart—that results in right deeds and right decisions.

> Righteousness as exemplified by Christ is not merely the absence of vice or the presence of virtue. It is a consuming passion for God which sends you forth in his name to establish his kingdom.
>
> IRVING PEAKE JOHNSON

Righteousness is right-ness. It means caring about what God cares about—in big things and little things too. It starts with belief—believing that God is who he says he is, that he will do what he says he will do. That's the first step in aligning your values with God's. And here's the amazing thing: From God's perspective, that first step—believing—doesn't just set you on the path toward righteousness. Believing is righteousness itself. One of the most incredible verses in the Bible is James 2:23: "Abraham believed God, so God declared him to be righteous" (NLT). If you have believed God, God has declared you righteous. You aren't perfect yet? True enough. But you've begun lining yourself up with God, and when God looks at you, he sees the righteous person that you are becoming. In you he sees the finished diamond, not just the lump of coal you see when you look in the mirror. So go out there and become what you have already become.

> How blessed are those who keep justice, Who practice righteousness at all times!
> Psalm 106:3 NASB

do something

Righteousness involves both an inside and an outside component. You're right with God spiritually—that is, God declares you righteous—and as a result, your outward works begin to reflect that inward righteousness. Righteousness always works its way from the inside out, not the other way around. Getting your outward works right won't make you spiritually right. But if you're lined up with God on the inside, that can't help but show on the outside.

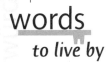

words
to live by

The kingdom of God is not food and drink but righteousness and peace and joy in the Holy Spirit.
Romans 14:17 NRSV

Whereas obedience is righteousness in relation to God, love is righteousness in relation to other people.
A. PLUMMER

⌐ The word *righteous* was originally spelled "rightwise"—similar to "crosswise" or "sidewise" (or sideways). Just as crosswise indicates that something or someone is aligned at cross-purposes, *rightwise* indicates that a person is aligned in the right direction.

⌐ Bible teachers distinguish between "imputed righteousness" and "progressive righteousness." *Imputed righteousness* is the righteousness of Christ applied to your account. God looks at you but sees Christ's righteousness. *Progressive righteousness* is the process by which your thoughts and actions begin to match up with those of Christ.

Final thought

God, you have declared me righteous. I pray that my actions would reflect that righteousness more and more. Amen.

sac·ri·fice, noun

1. the offering of some material possession to a deity.
2. the surrender or destruction of something prized or desir-able for the sake of a higher claim.
3. a loss incurred in selling something below its value.
4. **Biblical:** the offering of an animal or something else of value to God.
5. **Personal:** the act of giving up something of value in order to get something of greater value.

Give a little, Get a lot

I appeal to you therefore,
brothers and sisters, by the
mercies of God, to present your
bodies as a living sacrifice, holy
and acceptable to God, which is
your spiritual worship.
Romans 12:1 NRSV

It's the bottom of the ninth, and your team is down a run. The batter ahead of you in the lineup hits a lead-off double. You smile to yourself as you stroll from the on-deck circle toward the bat-ter's box. Get a hit, and you'll drive in the game-tying run. Maybe the next batter will drive you home for the heroic game-winning run. You can see yourself crossing the plate, greeted by all your teammates holding up their hands for high-fives. Better yet, maybe you can win the game with one home-run swing. Glory and acclaim, the wild applause of the home bleachers; you can hear it already.

Then you look down the third-base line to get your signal from the coach, and your blood runs cold. That's not the swing-away sign he's giving you. You look again. He's signaling for a sac-rifice bunt! He wants you to tap the ball down the first-base line,

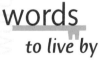

words
to live by

take your out, go sit down, and watch the next batter take all the glory for driving home the runner you bunted over to third.

A sacrifice bunt actually provides a good introduction to the biblical concept of sacrifice. To sacrifice is to give up something that's important to you. In the case of a sacrifice bunt, you're giving up your at-bat for somebody else, laying down your chance to get a hit, run the bases, be a hero. When an ancient Jew made a sacrifice at the temple, it had to be things of value— not a sick cow or a crippled lamb that would have to be killed anyway, but an animal that was worth something to the person making the sacrifice.

If my life is surrendered to God, all is well. Let me not grab it back, as though it were in peril in His hand but would be safer in mine!

ELISABETH ELLIOT

However, sacrifice is not merely a matter of giving things up. It's a matter of giving things up in order to gain something that's even better. If there's nobody on base and you bunt the ball back to the pitcher with no hope of getting to first, that's not a sacrifice, that's just bad baseball. It's only a sacrifice if you're giving up your at-bat in order to put your team in a position to score runs. Your at-bat is important to you, but contributing to the team's run tally is more important.

The world's most meaningful sacrifice was the death of God's own Son. Jesus was the Lamb of God, the perfect sacrifice who took away the world's sins once and for all. What made that sacrifice meaningful? It wasn't the greatness of what Jesus gave up that made his sacrifice great, though he gave up infinitely more than any mere human could. It was the greatness of what he gained that made his sacrifice great. He bought God's people back.

You are called to sacrifice too. Every day you are called to die to yourself. You are called to lay aside your own plans, your own glory so that you can serve others and lift up Christ. But it's not a loss. It's an investment. You die to self so that you can be alive to Christ. When you think of it that way, it doesn't seem like such a sacrifice after all.

> Like living stones, let yourselves be built into a spiritual house, to be a holy priesthood, to offer spiritual sacrifices acceptable to God through Jesus Christ.
> I Peter 2:5 NRSV

do something

The sacrifices you're called to make aren't usually great, heroic gestures. They're usually little things, like giving of your leisure time to visit the sick and elderly, sharing the Gospel when you'd rather just make small talk, giving your hard-earned money to a collection for the needy instead of spending it on yourself, spending part of your summer break on a missions project. That's how you make your life a living sacrifice.

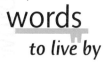

words
to live by

Even if my life is to be poured out like a drink offering to complete the sacrifice of your faithful service (that is, if I am to die for you), I will rejoice.

Philippians 2:17 NLT

That man is no fool who gives what he cannot keep to gain that which he cannot lose.

JIM ELLIOTT

A lot of ritual was involved in ancient Israel's temple sacrifice. But the Old Testament prophets frequently spoke out against those who thought they could get on God's good side by offering up animal sacrifices while their hearts were still far from God.

Once a year a single priest was chosen to enter the Holy of Holies and make a sacrifice on behalf of the Hebrew people. No one else was allowed in. He tied a rope around his leg so that if anything happened to him, the other priests could drag him out without having to go in after him

final thought

God, you sacrificed for me in ways that I can't even imagine. And yet I find it hard to give of myself even in little things sometimes. Forgive my selfishness. Make my life a living sacrifice. Amen.

sal·va·tion, noun

1. the act of saving from harm or loss.
2. the state of being thus saved.
3. a means of being thus saved.
4. **Biblical:** the deliverance from the power and penalty of sin.
5. **Personal:** God's rescue of sinners.

Bought for a Price

Here's a word you can take to heart
and depend on: Jesus Christ came into
the world to save sinners. I'm proof—
Public Sinner Number One.

1 Timothy 1:15 THE MESSAGE

A. J. Gordon, a Baptist preacher in Massachusetts during the late 1800s, was out for a walk one day when he saw a boy he knew carrying a birdcage. Inside the cage were several frightened-looking little brown birds. "Where did you get these birds?" Dr. Gordon asked.

"I trapped them out in the field," answered the boy.

"What do you plan to do with them?"

"Oh, I'll play with them for a little while, then I'll probably feed them to the cat."

Dr. Gordon felt a surge of pity for the little birds. They were made to fly free, but here they huddled terrified in the bottom of a rusty cage. They seemed to understand what a gloomy future lay before them.

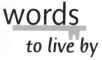

words
to live by

"Would you like to sell them?" the preacher asked.

The boy was surprised. There was nothing special about these little field birds. They didn't sing; they had no colorful plumage; they couldn't be taught to talk or to do anything else. But Dr. Gordon was serious about his offer, and he bought the birds and cage together for two dollars—not a small sum in the 1800s. When the boy was out of sight, Dr. Gordon opened the cage and let the birds go free. "That boy told me the birds weren't songsters," he told his congregation in a sermon the next Sunday, "but when I released them and they winged their way heavenward, it seemed to me they were singing "Redeemed, redeemed, redeemed!"

Christianity is the easiest religion in the world, because it is the only religion in which God does everything; it is the hardest religion because it robs us completely of being autonomous.

FRANCIS SHAEFFER

That's a great picture of salvation. Dr. Gordon bought those little birds in order to set them free. You, too, were bought with a price. On the cross, Jesus paid the ransom to set you free from the cage of sin and death.

Salvation is one of those religious words you hear so often that you almost forget it actually means something. Whenever you hear the word *salvation*, think "rescue." You can think of lots of situations where somebody is in need of rescue—a pilot shot down behind enemy lines, a mountain climber stuck on a rock face, a family in a burning house, a cat in a tree. What do all rescue scenarios have in common? In each case some-body's in a mess they can't get themselves out of. To be in need of rescue means you have lost the ability to act for yourself. And obviously, if you can't help yourself, some-body from the outside has to intervene in your situation if you hope to get out of it.

Jesus is the great Rescuer. Humankind didn't just need a little help getting themselves out of the hole of sin and death. They didn't need a few helpful tips that would allow them to figure out for themselves how to get out of the mess they were in. They needed a Savior, a Rescuer, just as surely as those caged birds needed someone to open the cage for them. Jesus bought you to set you free. Now fly.

> Restore to me the joy of Your salvation, and uphold me by Your generous Spirit.
> **Psalm 51:12** NKJV

do something

If you are still imprisoned by sin, turn to Jesus. You can't open the cage by yourself. You can't earn your way out or buy your way out. You need a Rescuer to get you out of the mess you were born into. Jesus has paid the ransom to set you free. Receive his gift, and fly away in freedom.

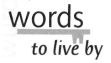

words
to live by

You have been bought
with a price: therefore
glorify God in your
body.
1 Corinthians 6:20 NASB

This is faith: a renounc-
ing of everything we
are apt to call our own
and relying wholly
upon the blood, righ-
teousness and interces-
sion of Jesus.
JOHN NEWTON

❧ Prior to Jesus' work of salvation, the most commonly used
biblical image of salvation was the
Exodus, when God delivered the
Hebrews from a life of slavery and
brought them up out of Egypt to
give them a land of their own, a
land flowing with milk and honey.

❧ You may think of the Salvation
Army as just a place to buy vintage
clothes, but it actually has a very
long history as a missionary organization, pointing the poor and
needy toward the salvation offered
by Christ.

Final thought

God, you bought me to give me my freedom. I will serve you
forever. Amen.

Sa·tan, noun

1. the chief evil spirit.
2. the devil.
3. the lord of evil.
4. **Biblical:** the great adversary of God and humankind; the Accuser, the Tempter, the Father of Lies.
5. **Personal:** the defeated enemy of God and his people, who remains a dangerous force on earth.

Dangerous, but Defeated

This is not a wrestling match against a human opponent. We are wrestling with rulers, authorities, the powers who govern this world of darkness, and spiritual forces that control evil in the heavenly world.

Ephesians 6:12 GOD'S WORD

You've probably seen movies where the villain receives a fatal wound but doesn't die for another minute or two. He staggers around the room, knocks things off tables, fires off whatever rounds are left in his gun, stumbles dangerously close to the detonator before finally collapsing in a heap. The villain can be quite dangerous in these situations. Good guys get hurt, even killed sometimes. Even when he's dying, the bad guy is determined to take as many people down with him as he can.

Satan's a lot like that dying bad guy. He received his death wound when Jesus died and rose again. But he won't be completely finished off until Judgment Day. In the meantime, he's dangerous. He's capable of causing all sorts of mayhem, even in the lives of Christians. He spreads lies, he levels false accusations, he snatches truth from people's hearts before it takes root, he

words
to live by

causes discord between friends and loved ones, he tempts people to sin.

Satan, according to the Scriptures, "prowls around like a roaring lion, seeking someone to devour" (1 Peter 5:8 NASB). Defeated already, he wants to take as many people down with him as he can. In the case of Christians, of course, he can't take them all the way down, but he can steal their joy. He can trick them into submitting to the slavery of sin and fear. Christ gives abundant life. Satan snatches it away. God is the Creator. Satan is the distorter. He can create nothing, only twist and pervert the good things that God has made. He doesn't really have any other tactics for attacking God. But he has become a master at it.

How, then, do you defend yourself against such a crafty and dangerous enemy? You're human; how can you do battle with spiritual forces? By taking the offensive. Satan has tremendous power to hurt those who fear him or who aren't ready for him. His tactics work especially well against people who don't believe in him. But he turns and runs from the person who fights back. "Resist the devil and he will flee from you" (James 4:7 NASB). How do you resist the devil? The next verse tells you: "Draw near to God and he will draw near to you" (James 4:8 NASB). That's the key: shoring up your relationship with God through

> There are two equal and opposite errors into which our race can fall about the devils. One is to disbelieve in their existence. The other is to believe, and to feel an excessive and unhealthy interest in them. They themselves are equally pleased by both errors, and hail a materialist or a magician with the same delight.
>
> **C. S. LEWIS**

Christ. You probably won't be "doing battle" with Satan in some dramatic showdown. You can leave that to God and his angels.

There's a battle between God and Satan, but you don't have to wonder what the outcome is going to be. Satan is a defeated foe. It's important to remember that even though Satan is powerful—frighteningly powerful— he's not God's equal. Before he fell from heaven, he was an angel, not a god, and he's still not a god. Yes, you should be on guard against Satan's attacks, but you don't need to be paralyzed with fear of Satan or his demons. You have God as your Protector. And as the Bible says, "Greater is He who is in you than he who is in the world" (1 John 4:4 NASB).

> Resist the Devil, and he will run away from you.
> **James 4:7** GNT

do something

Satan is a dangerous enemy. He has a whole bag of tricks for making people miserable. But he is a defeated enemy. You have everything you need to send him packing. If you're actively seeking God, Satan's ability to hurt you is severely restricted. If you're feeding daily on God's truth, Satan's lies will roll right off. If you're walking by the Spirit, Satan's temptations won't hold much appeal.

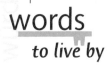

words
to live by

Put on the full armor of
God, so that you will be
able to stand firm
against the schemes of
the devil.
Ephesians 6:11 NASB

When the devil is called
the god of this world, it
is not because he made
it, but because we
serve him with our
worldliness.
SAINT THOMAS AQUINAS

The picture of the devil as a red
guy with horns, hooves, a tail, and
a pitchfork first appeared in the
Middle Ages. Because Satan's pet
sin is pride, Christians of that time
thought poking fun at Satan would
be a good way to combat him—
hence the ridiculous portraits.

Have you ever wondered
where the phrase "speak of the
devil" came from? It's a shortened
version of an old saying, "Speak of
the devil, and he will appear." It
refers to a superstition that merely
speaking of the devil would conjure him up.

Final thought

God, I am faced with a dangerous enemy—one I cannot defeat in my
own strength. But you are infinitely more powerful than he is, and
you are on my side. Draw near to me and be my great Guard. Amen.

ser·vant, noun

1. a person employed by another, especially one hired to per-form domestic duties.
2. a person in the service of another.
3. one who expresses submission, recognizance, or debt to another.
4. **Biblical:** one who voluntarily dedicates himself or herself to the service of another.
5. **Personal:** a person who is willing to put the interests and rights of another ahead of his or her own.

The Last Shall Be First

I am a free man, nobody's slave; but I make myself everybody's slave in order to win as many people as possible.

I Corinthians 9:19 GNT

It was a Thursday night. It had been a huge week for the disciples. On Sunday when they had gotten to town, the people of Jerusalem had greeted them like heroes. Actually, they greeted Jesus like a hero, but the disciples were right behind him, handling transportation, crowd control, the whole bit. It was a total mob scene—people throwing palm branches and even their cloaks in the road for Jesus' donkey to walk on, as if he were a general returning victorious from a military campaign.

By now, the disciples knew for sure that Jesus was the Messiah. The question was, when was he going to go public? The way things were going, they thought it might be any day now. As a matter of fact, Passover weekend was starting the next day; what better day to get out the word that the Messiah had arrived, that there was going to be a new man in charge around here.

words
to live by

The whole town was buzzing about Jesus—*What's his next move? Is he the Messiah or isn't he?* The disciples sort of liked being at the center of the buzz. When Jesus called the Twelve to a secret meeting, you could understand their excitement. It was all very hush-hush, in the upstairs room of some guy none of them even knew. Talk about being in the inner circle! Because, face it, if the Messiah overthrew the Romans and established the rule of God on earth, somebody would still have to run the government, right? He'd need a prime minister, chief of staff, secretary of state, secretary of transportation. And who better for the job than his twelve closest friends? Heaven knew they deserved a little recognition after all they'd put up with the last three years—trooping up one side of Palestine and down the other with no place to call home, constantly running into trouble with the local rabbis. But now, payday seemed just around the corner.

You know the generous act of our Lord Jesus Christ, that though he was rich, yet for your sakes he became poor, so that by his poverty you might become rich.

2 Corinthians 8:9 NRSV

Some of the disciples were arguing about which of them deserved the highest office in Jesus' new government when they noticed that Jesus had taken off his cloak and wrapped himself in a towel. He poured water in a basin, then stooped down and began washing the disciples' feet. It was a very uncomfortable moment. Only servants washed other people's feet—and only the lowest servants at that. Yet here was the Messiah wiping dust, mud, and camel manure from their feet.

our . grace mercy love faith goodness earth redeemed hope
forgiveness peace humble holiness obey repent perfect submit
erve fellowship comforter transformed noble character church

Peter was the first to speak up. He always was. "No," he said. "You will never wash my feet." But Jesus kept right on. Worldly rulers lord it over their subjects, Jesus explained, "But you are not to be like that. Instead, the greatest among you should be like the youngest, and the one who rules like the one who serves" (Luke 22:26 NIV). "Now that I, your Lord and Teacher, have washed your feet," he continued, "you also should wash one another's feet" (John 13:14 NIV).

It was the last evening the disciples would ever spend on earth with their servant-leader. The next day he went to usher in the kingdom of God—a kingdom where the first are last and the last first—by dying a servant's death on the cross.

> Even I, the Son of Man, came here not to be served but to serve others, and to give my life as a ransom for many.
> Matthew 20:28 NLT

do something

Do you want to be a leader? You'd better learn how to serve. Jesus makes it clear: if you aren't willing to stoop down and wash a person's feet, you aren't worthy to lead them. In the kingdom of God, leadership isn't about asserting your own rights; it's about asserting and protecting the rights of the people you hope to lead.

words
to live by

Now we who are strong ought to bear the weaknesses of those without strength and not just please ourselves.

Romans 15:1 NASB

A Christian man is the most free lord of all, and subject to none; a Christian man is the most dutiful servant of all, and subject to everyone.

MARTIN LUTHER

🔹 Some churches practice foot-washing as part of their worship services. They bring out basins of water and towels, members of the congregation take off their shoes, and they wash one another's feet as a sign of servanthood to one another.

🔹 The words translated *servant* in the New Testament—*doulos* and *diakonos*—both refer to a bond-slave, a person who is the purchased property of another. That's a pretty strong word to describe the service you owe to others, isn't it?

 **final thought**

God, give me the heart of a servant—a heart that looks for ways to meet the needs of others rather than asserting my own rights and privileges. Amen.

sin, noun

1. transgression of divine law.
2. any act regarded as such a transgression, especially a willful violation of some religious or moral principle.
3. something regarded as being shameful, deplorable, or utterly wrong.
4. *Biblical:* any disobedience of God's commands.
5. *Personal:* the act of stepping outside God's boundaries in an effort to get what you want.

If we confess our sins, He is faithful and righteous to forgive us our sins and to cleanse us from all unrighteousness.

1 John 1:9 NASB

A recent medical study linked "runner's high"—that feeling of well-being you get after an hour or so of exercise—with the buzz that comes from smoking marijuana. In both situations, the body has elevated levels of a chemical called *anandamide*. So is exercise just another drug? Is marijuana suddenly good for you, like running or biking? More to the point, what does this medical study have to do with a meditation on sin?

To answer that last question, forget about both exercise and marijuana for a minute. Focus instead on the end result of either one: the feeling of well-being. There's nothing wrong with that feeling. The desire to relieve stress and to feel happy and relaxed is a perfectly legitimate desire. The anandamide that your body produces isn't bad. It's God-given, designed to smooth out the anxiety that might otherwise paralyze you. What's so wrong, then,

words
to live by

about smoking pot? After all, it's just releasing God-given chemicals that your body releases anyway.

In the case of a runner's high, that good feeling is the by-product of an activity that builds up your whole self. It's as if your body is rewarding you for looking after it. You've got more energy, you think more clearly, your body feels stretched and limber. You feel good because you've done right by your body; the boost from the anandamide is just icing on the cake.

> Purify me from my sins, and I will be clean; wash me, and I will be whiter than snow. . . . Don't keep looking at my sins. Remove the stain of my guilt.
>
> **Psalm 51:7, 9 NLT**

Marijuana and other drugs short-circuit all that and skip straight to the good feeling. If you can get the good feeling without the hard work—without running or studying or interacting with other people—why bother with anything else? The problem is, drugs reduce a person's life to the mere pursuit of pleasure. It's a heartbreaking thing to watch people lose interest in everything that gives variety and richness to life, and narrow themselves down to the desire for the next high. But the high that was so thrilling the first time gets less and less satisfying, and soon addicts are numb even to the drug that is their one remaining desire.

You're probably not a drug addict. Nevertheless, the way drugs take over a person's life illustrates how sin of any kind takes over; drugs are just a more dramatic example. In the end, sin doesn't result from a desire for bad things. It results from trying to get good things—God-given things—in ways that go against God's plan for giving them to you. Robbing banks is a sin—not because God doesn't want you to have money, but because he wants you to have money as a by-product of work. Premarital sex is a sin—not because God doesn't want you to have sex, but because God designed sex to be the pinnacle of the intimacy and commitment of marriage.

There's a right way to get all the good things God offers in this life. Like a drug, sin promises that you can shortcut God's way and jump straight to the thing you want—security, well-being, intimacy, happiness, you name it. But sin never makes good on its promise. It lures you on to the next sin, then the next, in a futile effort to be satisfied. Worse yet, sin numbs you to the richness and variety—the abundance—of life lived God's way.

> All have sinned and fall short of the glory of God.
> **Romans 3:23** NKJV

do something

Whether you consciously think of it this way or not, you sin because you believe you're going to gain something from it. But you won't. Sin never keeps its promises. If there's a sin you're struggling with, try to identify what you're really hoping to gain from that sin. Then ask yourself, what is God's plan for giving that good thing to me?

words
to live by

Keep me safe, also, from willful sins; don't let them rule over me.
Psalm 19:13 GNT

It is not only that sin consists in doing evil, but in not doing the good that we know.
H. A. IRONSIDE

Saint Augustine on sin: "Sin arises when things that are a minor good are pursued as though they were the most important goals in life. . . . And that sin is magnified when, for these lesser goals, we fail to pursue the highest good and the finest goals."

A "sin of omission" is failing to do something that God commands you to do. A "sin of commission," on the other hand, is doing something that God commands you not to do. Sins of omission may not be as exciting as sins of commission, but they're still sins.

Final thought

God, I am a sinner. I've tried a lot of different ways to get the good things that only you can give. Forgive me. Restore me to a place where I can enjoy your gifts, your way. Amen.

soul, noun

1. the principle of life, feeling, thought, and action in a human being, regarded as a distinct entity separate from the body.
2. the emotional part of human nature; the seat of the feelings or sentiments.
3. a disembodied spirit of a deceased person.
4. *Biblical:* the spiritual nature in human beings.
5. *Personal:* the part of a human being that contains the image of God.

Who Are You?

God spoke: "Let us make human beings in our image, make them reflecting our nature."
Genesis 1:26 THE MESSAGE

Do you keep a Web log or an online journal? If you don't, you probably know someone who does. Of all the Web logs in existence, fifty-one percent are written by people between the ages of thirteen and nineteen. That's millions of teens making their thoughts and feelings available for friend and stranger alike. What's that all about? Why do people feel the need to shape their lives into short stories that can be typed up and posted on the Internet? Why do people feel the need to connect with other people through those stories? Why do people feel the need to leave their mark on the world, even if it's tucked away in an obscure corner of cyberspace?

Maybe it's because people have souls.

You were created in the image of God. That is to say, some

words
to live by

part of you bears a resemblance to the God who made you. What part is that? It's not your physical body, or any part of it. God, after all, doesn't have a body. It's your soul that bears the image of God. Sure, it's not a perfect likeness. Sometimes it's hardly recognizable. But every now and then, when the conditions are just right, the eternal breaks in on your everyday life and something inside you resonates like a tuning fork. That's your soul.

> The generous soul will be made rich, and he who waters will also be watered himself.
> **Proverbs 11:25** NKJV

You might say your soul is everything that separates your inner life from that of a monkey. Of course, it's hard to know what a monkey's inner life is like, since monkeys can't talk, but that's the point. Of the creatures on earth, only human beings have the ability to step outside themselves and talk about their inner lives. Only creatures with souls seek to connect with one another on a level beyond the connections that keep the species going. Only creatures with souls keep online journals or make art.

No scientific or psychological theory really explains art. There is no practical reason for a poem. There's no "point" in a painting. Except that the poet or the painter just couldn't help it; they had to create something. It's the image of God again, the human soul. God is the Creator. And the urge to create—even if it's only the urge to weld tractor parts into flower shapes or decorate your sneakers with a ballpoint pen—reflects God's creativity.

adness grace mercy love faith goodness truth freedom hope
orgiveness peace humble holiness obey repent perfect submit
erve fellowship comforter transformed noble character church

soul · soul · soul · soul · soul · soul · soul · soul

Blaise Pascal wrote, "There is a God-shaped vacuum in the heart of every man which cannot be filled by any created thing, but only by God, the Creator, made known through Jesus." Everybody has a soul, whether they realize it or not. In each of those souls is a longing to reconnect with the God who has stamped it with his image. Only genuine fellowship with God will do the trick. That's why the psalmists speak so exuberantly of their soul-filling communion with God. It's why they wrote so longingly of that fellowship when it was missing. Everybody tries to fit something into that God-shaped hole. But only God can fill it.

> As the deer pants for the water brooks, so my soul pants for You, O God. My soul thirsts for God, for the living God.
>
> Psalm 42:1–2 NASB

do something

You have a body and a soul. Your body lasts for a lifetime. Your soul lasts for an eternity. So which of the two do you think you should spend more time cultivating? Don't neglect the care of your soul. God is willing to fill that God-shaped place in your soul. Turn to him daily, and watch the image of God become clearer and clearer within you.

words
to live by

He satisfies the longing soul, and fills the hungry soul with goodness.
Psalm 107:9 NKJV

We take excellent care of our bodies, which we have for only a lifetime; yet we let our souls shrivel, which we will have for eternity.
BILLY GRAHAM

The word for *soul* in the Bible means literally "breath of life." When God shaped Adam's body from the dust, he then breathed life into his nostrils. That's the soul: the life-giving breath of God in you.

Some cultures used to believe that the soul could escape from the body when a person sneezed. This belief may have given rise to the tradition of saying "bless you" when a person sneezes.

final thought

God, your image is stamped on my soul. Restore your image. Fill me up. Amen.

suc·cess, noun

1. the favorable or prosperous conclusion of attempts or endeavors.
2. the attainment of wealth, position, or honors.
3. a person who achieves goals.
4. **Biblical:** the hoped-for outcome of one's efforts.
5. **Personal:** the state of being used by God to do God's work.

Let the kindness of the Lord our God be with us. Make us successful in everything we do. Yes, make us successful in everything we do.
Psalm 90:17 GOD'S WORD

Do you feel like a success? Whether you answer yes or no to that question, give some thought to what the Bible says about God's opinion of worldly success. This is Paul writing to the people of the Corinthian church:

"Take a good look, friends, at who you were when you got called into this life. I don't see many of 'the brightest and the best' among you, not many influential, not many from high-society families. Isn't it obvious that God deliberately chose men and women that the culture overlooks and exploits and abuses, chose these 'nobodies' to expose the hollow pretensions of the 'somebodies'?" (1 Corinthians 1:26–28 THE MESSAGE).

There God goes again, doing the exact opposite of what you'd expect. If you really want to get a message out, doesn't it make

words
to live by

more sense to use celebrities, who already have a built-in audience, or millionaires, who have the money to fund evangelism programs, or politicians, who could pass laws requiring people to attend church?

That's not how God chose to build his Church. He chose to use regular people, who weren't unusually well-educated, unusually wealthy, or unusually influential. And through them, the gospel spread like wildfire. This was the same God, remember, who came to earth not as a conquering king or general leading vast armies against his enemies, but as a baby born to a lowly carpenter and his teenage wife. He never held a government office. He never ran a company. He never even owned a home.

Duty is ours;
results are God's.
JOHN QUINCY ADAMS

Consider the case of Edward Kimball. You've probably never heard of him. But through him, hundreds of millions of people heard the gospel, and many thousands came to Christ. Kimball was a Sunday school teacher in Boston. In 1855, he led one of his teenage students to Christ. That student was Dwight L. Moody, who became one of the greatest evangelists of all time—the Billy Graham of his day. God used an undistinguished but faithful Sunday school teacher to put Dwight L. Moody on the right path. It's easy to recognize Moody as a success, with his huge evangelistic meetings and thousands of converts. But in the big scheme of things, wasn't Edward Kimball just as successful?

God gives success a new definition. The world defines success in terms of things like wealth, titles, and winning. For God,

indness grace mercy love faith goodness truth forgiveness hope
graiveness peace humble holiness obey repent perfect submit
serve fellowship comforter transformed noble character church

success is about touching the lives of other people, building his Church, bringing the kingdom of God to bear on the kingdoms of the world. That may result in what the world calls success, and it might not. It's not that God can't or won't use people who enjoy worldly success. He's used kings, millionaires, sports heroes, entertainers, and other successful people all over the world. God may see fit to give you that kind of success. You might find a cure for cancer someday. You might be valedictorian, or captain of the soccer team. Strive to be your best, whatever you turn your energies to. But when you achieve success (or, for that matter, if you never feel you do), remember that everything you have, everything you've achieved comes from God. As Paul told the Corinthians: "If you're going to blow a horn, blow a trumpet for God" (1 Corinthians 1:31 THE MESSAGE).

> With me [Wisdom] are riches and honor, enduring wealth and prosperity. My fruit is better than fine gold; what I yield surpasses choice silver.
>
> **Proverbs 8:18–19** NIV

do something

Everybody wants to succeed. The question is, how do you define success, and why do you want it? For a Christian, to be successful is to be used by God to do God's work. In other words, success isn't all about you. Sure, you may be blessed with what the world calls success. Thank God for it, then ask yourself, "How can this so-called success be transformed into the true success of being used by God?"

Since a dull ax requires great strength, sharpen the blade. That's the value of wisdom; it helps you succeed.
Ecclesiastes 10:10 NLT

No matter how difficult the challenge, when we spread our wings of faith and allow the winds of God's Spirit to lift us, no obstacle is too great to overcome.
ROY LESSIN

Alexander the Great, the Macedonian military genius, conquered the known world, from Egypt to India. Yet it is said that he cried when he realized he had no more countries left to conquer. His earthly success was staggering, but in the end it didn't satisfy him.

President James Garfield once headed a college. In response to a father asking about a shortcut for his son, Garfield said, "When God wants to make an oak tree, He takes a hundred years. When He wants to make a squash he requires only two months."

final thought

God, bring me success in everything I do—the success of being used by you. If that looks like success to the world, I give you glory. If it looks like failure, I give you the glory then too. Amen.

Be a Winner

temp·ta·tion, noun

1. the act of persuading a person to do something regarded as unwise or wrong.
2. a thing that entices.
3. the fact or state of being enticed or lured.
4. **Biblical:** a test or trial of a person's character.
5. **Personal:** a moment of choice—whether to obey God and win a victory, or disobey God and fail the test.

Cuddling a Rattlesnake

God, who faithfully keeps his promises, will not allow you to be tempted beyond your power to resist. But when you are tempted, he will also give you the ability to endure the temptation as your way of escape.

1 Corinthians 10:13 GOD'S WORD

There's an old Indian story about a young brave who had climbed a mountain to hunt on a cold winter's day. When he got to the top, he was surprised to see a rattlesnake coiled beside a stump. The brave walked over with careful steps to see if it was alive. He heard a hissing, then realized the snake was talking. "Pleas-s-se," said the snake in a whisper barely audible over the stiff mountain breeze, "Pleas-s-se, could you warm me under your cloak and carry me back down the mountain where I belong?"

The brave was none too sure about that. "But your tribe has ever been an enemy to my tribe," he said. "I am afraid you would bite me."

"Pleas-s-se . . ." hissed the snake. "I'm freezing. I am nearly dead. How could I harm you? Your cloak is warm, and you are

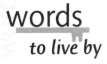

words
to live by

strong. What could it hurt for you to carry me to the warm valley and safety?"

The young brave's mother had always told him that only a fool would trust a rattlesnake. But this one seemed sincere enough. The snake spoke so convincingly. The look in his slitted eyes was so pitiful. And his scales were so beautiful. In spite of his qualms, the brave picked up the snake and put it under his cloak to warm while he carried it down the mountain. When they reached the valley below, he reached into his cloak and pulled the snake out. To his horror, the snake—now warmed and feeling more itself again—sank its fangs into his forearm. Shocked, the brave stumbled backward a step and asked in a hurt voice, "Why did you do that? You have deceived me!"

No man knows how bad he is until he has tried to be good. There is a silly idea about that good people don't know what temptation means.

C. S. Lewis

"Deceived you?" hissed back the rattlesnake. "I never deceived you. You knew I was a rattlesnake when you picked me up."

Rarely does a temptation come up and say, "Ps-s-st . . . want to do something wrong?" Temptation is usually more subtle. It says things like, "How would you like to have some fun?" or "Who's it going to hurt if you . . ." or "You don't want to look like a judgmental jerk, do you?" Temptation always says what you want to hear. Do you need an excuse to do the wrong thing? Temptation always has one close at hand. Do you want to be able to deny responsibility? Fine. Whatever. When you get bitten, you can say, "Gosh, how was I supposed to know. . . ?"

But the truth is almost always the same: You knew what it was when you picked it up.

Here's the good news about temptation: God never allows you to be tempted beyond your ability to resist. "But when you are tempted, he will also provide a way out" (1 Corinthians 10:13 NIV). The way out, by the way, is often a door. A real door. Resisting temptation is often as easy as leaving the place where you're being tempted: the party, the car, the Web site. Of course, you can always find a reason not to leave if you're not serious about resisting temptation. According to the Bible, there's no such thing as actually being overcome by temptation. Every single temptation you face is an opportunity for victory. Every time you walk away from a temptation, you look a little more like Jesus.

> Stay alert; be in prayer so you don't wander into temptation without even knowing you're in danger.
> **Matthew 26:41** THE MESSAGE

do something

Some temptations really do sneak up on you. It's against those temptations that you pray in the Lord's Prayer "lead us not into temptation." But how often do you lead yourself into temptation? How often do you put yourself in situations where you know you'll be tempted to disobey God? That's something you have control over. It's up to you to avoid the places, people, and situations that you know cause you to stumble.

words
to live by

Because [Jesus] himself suffered when he was tempted, he is able to help those who are being tempted.
Hebrews 2:18 NIV

Temptation is not a sin; it is a call to battle.
ERWIN W. LUTZER

Peirazo, along with its various forms, is the New Testament word for "tempt." It literally means "to test, try, prove," in a good way. Temptation is a test, and, like any test, it's good if you pass, and bad if you fail.

In the darkest reaches of the ocean, the anglerfish tempts its prey with a glowing lure, dangling just inches in front of its terrifying, snapping teeth. Fish are attracted to the glow, the only light around, but when they get close enough to investigate—you can guess what happens.

final thought

God, thank you that you never let me face a temptation that I can't escape. Thank you for giving me the grace to walk away. Amen.

thank·ful·ness, noun

1. grateful acknowledgment of gifts or favors.
2. expression of thanks, especially to God.
3. a feeling of gratitude for a benefit or favor.
4. *Biblical:* a spirit of appreciation for gifts and blessings received, especially from God.
5. *Personal:* the habit of being constantly aware of the blessings in your life.

A Healthy Habit

In everything give thanks; for this is God's will for you in Christ Jesus.

I Thessalonians 5:18 NASB

You're sitting amid a pile of birthday presents. The party was great. But now everybody's gone, the wrapping paper's in the trash can, and you're faced with the daunting task of thank-you notes. Gloom settles over you like a fog. You suddenly wish you hadn't invited so many friends to your birthday party. Thankfulness—what a chore.

Thankfulness sometimes feels like an afterthought, coming at the tail end of an exchange, after all the real excitement is over. Think about when you were a kid—your mom nudged you after the nice man handed you an ice-cream cone: "Now what do you say, honey?" You were already halfway through the cone. You look up and mumble through a mouthful of ice cream, "Huh? . . . Oh . . . yeah . . . Thanks." Some people never outgrow the tendency to forget to say thank you. That's too bad. Because a thankful heart is one of the keys to a joy-filled life.

words
to live by

To give thanks is to acknowledge and appreciate the fact that somebody else, whether God or another person, has played a part in making you happy. Somebody has given of their resources or themselves to build you up. To say thanks is to build a bridge between you and a person who has done good to you. For that reason alone, it's good and right to give thanks.

> Seeing our Father in everything makes life one long thanksgiving and gives a rest of heart.
> HANNAH WHITALL SMITH

But as thankfulness becomes habitual, you find that there are greater benefits—benefits that permeate your whole life. What is habitual thanks? Think of it this way: When a child is first learning to say thanks, that thanks is always linked to a specific event or occasion. You might call it occasional thanks. The child receives a gift, the child says thanks for the gift. The child gets a cookie, the child says thanks for the cookie. Gratitude, in that case, is always looking backward, paying back small kindnesses with words of thanks. That's a good way for a child to begin moving toward a habit of thanksgiving. But the child's not there yet.

Habitual thanks results from a constant awareness that everything in your life is a gift from God. If you see everything as a gift, words of thanks are always on your tongue, looking for any excuse to come out and express themselves. If occasional thanks looks backward, habitual thanks looks around, searching out the good in every situation, ready to give thanks to God or to other people.

The great enemy of thankfulness is selfishness. A selfish heart takes what it can get, then closes back up. Thankfulness, on the other hand, opens the heart wider and wider. And an open heart is more ready to receive future blessings. Or you could think of it this way: Selfishness creates a crust over your heart, like the hard-packed dirt of an unplowed field. God's blessings roll right off. Thankfulness breaks through like a garden tiller, preparing the ground of your heart and allowing the showers of God's blessings to soak through.

> It is good to give thanks to the Lord, to sing praises to your name, O Most High.
> Psalm 92:1 NRSV

do something

The Bible says it's God's will for you to be thankful in all things. A habit of thanksgiving makes it easier to see what's worthy of thanks, whatever the situation. Nevertheless, there are times when even the most thankful person can't see the good in a situation. Even then, you can thank God for the promise that he will redeem even that situation and bring good out of it somehow.

words
to live by

Everything that God has created is good; nothing is to be rejected, but everything is to be received with a prayer of thanks.

I Timothy 4:4 GNT

The unthankful heart . . . discovers no mercies; but the thankful heart . . . will find, in every hour, some heavenly blessing.

HENRY WARD BEECHER

A notorious freeloader was staying at a friend's estate. His friend said, "The servants expect tips. Knowing you were short on cash, I gave them three dollars each and said it was from you." "Three dollars?" said the unthankful houseguest. "It should have been five. They'll think I'm a cheapskate."

A pastor named Sydney Smith sent this thank-you note to a church member who gave him some fresh strawberries: "What is real piety? What is true attachment to the Church? How are these fine feelings best evinced? The answer is plain: by sending strawberries to a clergyman. Many thanks."

final thought

God, give me a heart full of thanks, so that I might see the blessings that surround me and be ready to receive them. Amen.

A Healthy Habit

wis·dom, noun

1. knowledge of what is true and right coupled with good judgment.
2. scholarly knowledge or learning.
3. wise sayings or teachings.
4. **Biblical:** understanding, both in spiritual and earthly matters, that comes from God.
5. **Personal:** the ability to choose long-term joy over immediate pleasure.

How Much Wisdom Do You Want?

If any of you lacks wisdom, he should ask God, who gives generously to all without finding fault, and it will be given to him.

James 1:5 NIV

The kindergartner ponders his choice. On the table in front of him, the nice lady with the clipboard has placed a small candy bar—the mini-size kind that people put in your trick-or-treat bag. The lady says he can eat it now if he wants to. Or he can wait half an hour, and she'll bring him a full-size candy bar if he hasn't eaten this little one. That's a tough choice for a kindergartner. He gets the concept that a big candy bar is better than a little candy bar. But still, at this point the big candy bar is just a theory. That little candy bar is right here where he can see it, touch it, rattle the wrapper. He doesn't doubt the clipboard lady would make good on her promise, but half an hour does seem a long time to wait for a theoretical candy bar when there's a real one right here.

If you've ever taken a psychology course, you might remember this experiment. It's the classic illustration of delayed gratifi-

words
to live by

cation. (And in case you're wondering, kindergartners take the little candy bar about 70 to 75 percent of the time). It might just as easily be called a wisdom experiment, because wisdom always seems to involve a choice between immediate gratification and big-picture, long-term happiness. A wise person sees what's going to bring deep, lasting happiness, and that vision gives the person the ability to pass up fleeting pleasures that might get in the way of that happiness. This applies to spiritual and earthly matters equally.

> Do not worry about what you do not understand. . . . Worry about what you do understand in the Bible but do not live by.
>
> **CORRIE TEN BOOM**

You may have already started receiving credit card offers. If you haven't yet, you will by the time you finish your first semester of college. Here is the promise of immediate happiness. You want something? Go get it. You can worry about paying for it later. Hm . . . that was easy. So you go get something else. The problem is, "later" comes eventually, and you've thrown away your financial freedom for the sake of some clothes that are already out of style and electronic equipment that already looks like something Abraham Lincoln would have used. It's the same way when you unwisely fall for any other kind of temptation: Long after the pleasure is forgotten, you're still paying the price.

One of the great things about wisdom is that God promises to give it freely to anyone who asks for it. As the writer Alexander Maclaren pointed out, God puts the key to his treasure room in your hands: "If a man is admitted into the bullion vault of a bank and told to help himself, and comes out with one cent, whose fault is it that he is poor?" You can be as wise as you want to be. It doesn't take a lot of education. It doesn't take a lot of consultants. It takes vision—the vision to see the difference between what will give you joy and what will take it away. And God gives it freely. So how much wisdom do you want?

> Wisdom is better than rubies, and all the things one may desire cannot be compared with her.
> **Proverbs 8:11** NKJV

do something

The Bible calls you to walk by faith, not by sight. Many times, an unwise choice comes from focusing on what you can see—walking by sight—and missing what can be perceived only by faith. Like that kindergartner in the experiment, who latched on to the little candy bar he could see because he had trouble imagining the big candy bar he couldn't see. Wisdom takes imagination—the imagination that comes from faith.

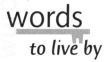

words
to live by

Oh, what a wonderful God we have! How great are his riches and wisdom and knowledge! How impossible it is for us to understand his decisions and his methods!
Romans 11:33 NLT

Wisdom is the right use of knowledge. To know is not to be wise. . . . There is no fool so great a fool as a knowing fool. But to know how to use knowledge is to have wisdom.
CHARLES H. SPURGEON

If Philippians is the joy book and Psalms is the praise book, Proverbs is the wisdom book. Written by King Solomon, the world's wisest man, the word *wise* in all its forms appears 125 times in the thirty-one chapters of Proverbs.

The Greek word for wisdom is *sophia. Sophia* is the root for the word "philosophy," the love of wisdom. It's also the first root for the word *sophomore*, which means, literally, "wise fool" or "wise moron."

 **final thought**

God, you say you'll grant wisdom to anyone who asks for it. Well, I'm asking. I need the wisdom that only you can give. I can't afford to walk by mere sight any longer. Amen.

work, noun

1. exertion or effort directed to produce or accomplish some thing.
2. a task or undertaking.
3. employment, as in some form of industry, especially as a means of earning one's livelihood.
4. **Biblical:** the act of making, doing, or creating, especially in employments to which one is called by God.
5. **Personal:** your earthly employments.

God is the Boss

Whatever you do, work at it with all your heart, as working for the Lord, not for men.

Colossians 3:23 NIV

You might have a summer job or an after-school job. If so, what motivates you to do good work? It's probably not the money. You've probably noticed that your co-workers who do mediocre work—just enough not to get fired—draw a paycheck just like you do. So even though money is a reason to get a job, it's not always sufficient motivation to do your job well. Fear of the boss is one reason to do good work, but it's not a very good reason. There's always a time when the boss isn't looking and won't know whether you've done good work or not. Is it love of your customers that keeps you doing your best work? That's getting closer to a good motivation, but customers can be unlovable at times. Some of them are a little too literal in their interpretation of the saying "the customer is always right."

words
to live by

There are lots of motivators for doing good work, some better than others. But the Bible offers the only perfect motivation: "Whatever you do, do it with all your heart, as working for the Lord, not for men." Ultimately, God is your boss, at work and at school no less than at church. This is his world—all of it. Your church is no more sacred than the McDonald's where you landed a job taking orders at the drive-through. Your quiet time is no more sacred than the time you've committed to stocking shelves at the grocery store or doing your homework. Don't take that the wrong way: That doesn't mean you're free to skip church and sleep through your quiet time because you're glorifying God at work and school. School and work would get out of whack pretty quickly if you did that. But on the other hand, the spirituality you practice at church and in your quiet time wouldn't mean very much if it didn't shape your life at work and school.

> The discovery of God lies in the daily and the ordinary, not in the spectacular and the heroic. If we cannot find God in the routines of home and shop, then we will not find Him at all.
> **Richard J. Foster**

What does it mean to be "working for God and not for men"? It means you do your best to look like Christ in your workplace. You're honest, never cheating customers or your employer. That may seem like an obvious one, but consider how common it is for employees to steal time that their employer is paying for—showing up a few minutes late, leaving a few minutes early, taking fifteen minutes for a ten-minute break. Integrity in those little areas is a real testimony.

Likewise, submitting to the authority of your boss is another great testimony. God put people in authority over you. And unless they're asking you to do something unethical, follow their leadership cheerfully. That's not something managers see a lot of. Serve your co-workers. Do more than your share. And do your job as well as you can do it. If you work at a car wash, make sure your chrome is as shiny as it can be. Not only does it show you consider your work to be important, it shows you consider your customers and co-workers to be important too.

The irony is that when you work to please God rather than people, you please people more than ever. You succeed in your work, to the glory of God.

> Our people should also learn how to set an example by doing good things when urgent needs arise so that they can live productive lives.
>
> **Titus 3:14** GOD'S WORD

do something

So you've got a job flipping burgers? Great. Because you've got co-workers who need to see what Jesus would look like flipping burgers. He'd do it without complaining. He'd do it with a genuine interest in the lives of his co-workers and the well-being of the customers who will eat his burgers. He'd do it cheerfully. And he'd pull the fries out at just the right moment—not too soft, not too crispy.

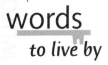

words
to live by

Richard J. Foster wrote this about work: "The discovery of God lies in the daily and the ordinary, not in the spectacular and the heroic. If we cannot find God in the routines of home and shop, then we will not find Him at all."

Even when they were still living in the Garden of Eden, before sin entered the world, Adam and Eve had work to do in the Garden. Work is a good thing, not a curse. It was part of God's plan for human happiness even before the Fall.

Even while we were with you, we gave you this rule: "Whoever does not work should not eat."
2 Thessalonians 3:10
NLT

One can understand what play is only when one also understands what work is.
KARL BARTH

final thought

God, this whole world is yours; you pour significance into everything in it. In my schoolwork and in my job, give me eyes to see that it all has meaning when I offer it up to you. Amen.

God Is the Boss

wor·ry, noun

1. a state of disturbance from care or anxiety.
2. something or someone that causes anxiety; a source of unhappiness.
3. **Biblical:** a state of distress caused by anxiety about the future, resulting from a failure or inability to trust in God's care.
4. **Personal:** self-inflicted torture resulting from carrying concerns about the future that you were not made to carry.

Be anxious for nothing, but in everything by prayer and supplication, with thanksgiving, let your requests be made known to God.
Philippians 4:6 NKJV

Class is about to start. The bell has already rung, and the stragglers are finding their seats. You're wondering what's happened to the friend who usually sits in the desk beside you when you see him come through the door staggering under the weight of a huge backpack. It's not a regular school backpack, but one of those big hiking packs with a frame. And it's obviously loaded down with something heavy. Your friend knocks over two desks and a sophomore as he sidles down the aisle to the seat beside you. The pack falls to the floor with a thud, and your friend sighs as he sits down.

"Where have you been?" you whisper.

He gestures toward the pack. "Lugging that thing. It's slow going, let me tell you." You're intrigued.

When class is over, your friend struggles to get the pack up

words
to live by

on his shoulders. "Hey, wait up," he calls. You help lift the pack; it weighs a ton.

"What's in the pack?" you ask, trying to sound as nonchalant as possible.

"Rocks."

You think on that a few seconds. "And why are you carrying around a sack of rocks?"

"Because you never know when you might need a rock."

You try to think of a time you might need a rock, but nothing springs to mind. "Like when?" you ask.

> Any concern too small to be turned into a prayer is too small to be made into a burden.
> **CORRIE TEN BOOM**

"Like if a bear attacked."

"In the school building?"

Your friend looks at you as if you've lost your mind. "Hello? Of course not in the school building. But what if we were outside and a bear attacked us? You'd be glad I was prepared with rocks to throw at him."

"But if we were outside and we needed rocks, couldn't we just pick some up?"

"Anyway," your friend says, changing the subject, "my knees are killing me. You have no idea what it's like to lug this thing around all day."

"Then don't," you suggest. "Nobody's making you, are they?"

"No," he answers, a little defensively. "But still, you never know when you'll need some rocks."

"Why don't you put the rocks down," you say. "There's no point in carrying them around, and you'll feel a lot better." He agrees eventually, so you help him off with the pack. "There, isn't that better?"

"It sure is," he replies, rubbing his sore shoulders. "Lots better."

You resume your walk to your next class, at a quicker pace now. But you notice your friend isn't beside you. He's back where you left him, struggling to get that pack of rocks back on his shoulders.

It would be hard to have patience with a person who took that kind of debilitating burden on themselves for no good reason, especially if he kept complaining about it. Yet it happens all the time. A load of worry can crush you. But it's a load you can throw off any time you want to. The great majority of things you worry about never happen. And even when the thing you worry about does happen, the worry didn't help matters any. Your future is in the hands of a good God. You weren't made for worry. You were made for faith. Let it go.

> Anxiety weighs down the human heart, but a good word cheers it up.
>
> **Proverbs 12:25 NRSV**

do something

The Bible offers a pretty simple solution to worry and anxiety: pray. You were never meant to carry a pack of rocks around with you. That kind of self-punishment serves no purpose. Worse than that, it demonstrates a lack of faith in God, who has everything under control. So hand those worries over to God. He can handle them. You've got a life to live.

words
to live by

When anxiety was great within me, your consolation brought joy to my soul.
Psalm 94:19 NIV

Pray, and let God worry.
MARTIN LUTHER

The English word *worry* originally meant "to choke or strangle." Isn't that the perfect picture of what worry does to you? Worrying is like choosing to be choked or strangled. It squeezes the joy out of your life.

Ian Maclaren on worry: "God gives us the power to bear all the sorrow of His making, but He does not guarantee to give us strength to bear the burdens of our own making such as worry induces."

final thought

God, I know I've got nothing to worry about. I know you've got everything under control. But worry is such a habit. Help me to break the habit, and transform those worries into prayers. Amen.